Barbecues & Grills

DAVID & CHARLES

Newton Abbot London

British Library Cataloguing in Publication Data
Barbecues & grills.—(David & Charles Kitchen Workshop)
  1. Barbecue cookery
  I. Grillmat. *English*
  641.7′6   TX840.B3

ISBN 0-7153-8480-5

© Text: David & Charles 1983
   Colour illustrations: A/S Hjemmet 1981
   Line illustrations: A/S Hjemmet 1981

Filmset by MS Filmsetting, Frome, Somerset
and printed in The Netherlands
by Smeets Offset BV, Weert
for David & Charles (Publishers) Limited
Brunel House, Newton Abbot, Devon

Using the Barbecue

To cook your food over an open fire is the oldest and simplest method of preparing raw ingredients – and the best, according to many people.
If, however, you are unable to cook food in this way and are tempted by the recipes in this book, all the recipes can be followed using the grill of a conventional domestic cooker.

The Barbecue

This can be a simple iron grid placed across a few stones. It can also be a hyper-technical appliance with a motor-operated spit, copper hood, built-in fish board and wine rack. Between these extremes there are other models – large, small, fixed and portable – in a varied price range.

When buying a barbecue there are a few things one should consider carefully. For instance, how is it going to be used, and how often? How much room is available in the garden or on a balcony or patio? How many are we going to cook for in one go – just the family, or guests as well? And finally, but importantly, how much money are we willing to spend?

For someone who is just a novice in the art of grilling, it is sensible to start with a simple, but strong, barbecue with a portable grid. The size depends on individual needs. There are small, excellent ones on the market made of cast iron with one or two loose grids. This type is meant for grilling on the balcony, or when you go camping. If you are using the barbecue in the garden, it is sensible to choose one with sturdy legs and a wind shield.

If you are going to grill large chunks of meat (eg a whole leg of lamb) it is advisable to choose a barbecue with a rotating spit, either manual or motor-operated.

The bottom of the barbecue must be strong enough to withstand the heat created when grilling. Furthermore, it should be deep enough to allow room for charcoal or briquettes, in sufficient quantity for 2–3 hr of cooking.

Accessories

The grill tongs are an important tool. One should never pierce the skin of meat or fish when turning it, therefore always use tongs.

Among other practical accessories are a basting brush, large and small barbecue skewers, a palette knife or fish slice with a long handle to use for fish, sandwiches etc. Thick oven gloves are a must, as well as a shovel with a long handle to heap up and spread the coals. A sprinkling bottle with water should always be kept nearby. Fat dripping from meat and fish can ignite from time to time, and the flames can be extinguished by means of a sprinkling bottle.

Lighting the Barbecue

If you are going to move the barbecue after use, it is sensible to place a thick sheet of tinfoil, shiny side facing up, at the bottom of the barbecue. The foil causes the heat to be thrown back against the grill grid and also makes it easier to gather up the ashes after use.

In a stationary barbecue, cover the bottom with a layer of rough gravel. This gives a good draught and you can leave the ashes in between using. To light, use sticks and paper with special solid fuel tablets, and over this a layer of charcoal mixed with briquettes. Never use ordinary fire-lighters or dangerous liquids such as paraffin or petrol. They can flare and will give a bad flavour to the food.

The amount of charcoal to use depends on what you are grilling. Large slices of meat take longer to grill and therefore use more charcoal.

The barbecue is ready for use when the coals are covered by a thin layer of grey ash – this takes about 30–45 min, depending on how thick the layer of charcoal is. Never start grilling if there are still visible flames – wait until the coals are grey. Brush grid with oil to prevent the food from sticking to it, although if the grid is made of enamel, this is not necessary.

Extinguishing the Barbecue

The barbecue should *always* be extinguished before leaving. In a strong, stationary grill, positioned far away from trees, bushes, house walls, roof extensions and such like, you might perhaps allow the coals to burn themselves out, but there will always be a danger of fire. Portable grills should always be completely extinguished with water from the sprinkling bottle. If the barbecue is used on the beach or when camping, it is a good rule always to cover the bottom with thick tinfoil. Sprinkle coals well with water and wrap the wet coals in the tinfoil after extinguishing.

Ingredients, Marinades and Oils

Nearly all meat, fish etc which can be fried in a pan, can be barbecued or grilled. Here you will find out more about the foods best suited to this process, and about marinades and oils.

SUITABLE RAW MATERIALS

Everything to be barbecued should be of best quality. Fish and shellfish should be fresh and firm. If you use frozen food it must be defrosted completely and dried well, but fresh raw materials will always give a better result than frozen ones. Beef should have been well hung and all meat should be from tender cuts. Avoid fatty meat, as the fat will melt and drip onto the coals, which may then flare up. In any case you will get smoke.

All raw materials must be dried well before being brushed with oil or placed in a marinade, which is often used for brushing.

Nearly everything can be grilled, whether we grill it on the grid itself, on skewers placed on the grid or in a grill net or rack.

Here are a few suggestions:

Steaks   all varieties, also 'steaks' made from pork and beef mince
Chops   beef, pork and lamb
Fillet   beef and pork
Ribs   (spare ribs) – lamb and pork
Schnitzels   pork
Chicken   cut in 2, 4 or 8 pieces
Sausages   all varieties
Offal   liver, kidney and heart
Sandwiches   double with filling in between
Vegetables and Fruit   nearly all types

Large Slices of Meat   whole roasts and whole chickens can be grilled on a rotating spit. Place a tinfoil dish underneath to catch all the drips, and bank the coals around it.

MARINATING

Meat and fish are often marinated before being cooked. The acid in the marinade – from the wine, vinegar, lemon juice etc, – tenderises the meat fibres. It also gives the unmistakable spicy flavour of barbecued food.

The marinade is carefully wiped off the meat or fish before grilling on either grid or skewer. You can also brush the food with marinade while it is cooking.

Special marinades have been listed in many of the recipes.

Basic marinades, suitable for most types of fish and meat, are listed below:

Beef

Mix 4–5 × 15ml tbsp (4–5tbsp) red wine with 3 × 15ml tbsp (3tbsp) oil, 1 small sliced onion and 4 coarsely crushed peppercorns. Add $\frac{1}{2}$ × 5ml tsp ($\frac{1}{2}$tsp) dried thyme or $\frac{1}{2}$ chopped bay leaf.

Pork

Mix 3–4 × 15ml tbsp (3–4tbsp) oil with 1–2 × 15ml tbsp (1–2tbsp) lemon juice, dry white wine or sherry, 2 coarsely crushed, black peppercorns and 2–3 sprigs of parsley. You can also add either 1 crushed garlic clove, 1 × 5ml tsp (1tsp) mustard, 1 × 15ml tbsp (1tbsp) tomato purée or 1–2 × 5ml tsp (1–2tsp) soy sauce.

Lamb

Mix 4 × 15ml tbsp (4tbsp) oil with 2 × 15ml tbsp (2tbsp) lemon juice or 1 × 15ml tbsp (1tbsp) white wine vinegar, 1 crushed garlic clove, 3 crushed peppercorns, $\frac{1}{2}$–1 × 5ml tsp ($\frac{1}{2}$–1tsp) dried rosemary and 1 sprig of parsley. Add either $\frac{1}{2}$ × 5ml tsp ($\frac{1}{2}$tsp) dried thyme or 1 × 15ml tbsp (1tbsp) grated lemon rind.

Poultry

Mix 3–4 × 15ml tbsp (3–4tbsp) oil with 1 × 15ml tbsp (1tbsp) lemon juice or dry white wine, 1 finely chopped onion, 3 crushed peppercorns and 3 sprigs of fresh tarragon or parsley.

Fish

Mix 3–4 × 15ml tbsp (3–4tbsp) oil with 2 × 15ml tbsp (2tbsp) lemon juice or 1 × 15ml tbsp (1tbsp) white wine vinegar, 2 crushed peppercorns, 1 sprig fresh dill or a little fresh fennel or $\frac{1}{2}$ × 5ml tsp ($\frac{1}{2}$tsp) dried fennel seeds.

Game

Same marinade as for beef, but add 3–4 crushed juniper berries.

BARBECUE OILS

There are used for brushing meat, fish or vegetables while grilling. You can buy various types of barbecue oils with different flavours. Some of them are tasty, but expensive. It is therefore more economical to mix you own. Make one for meat, another for fish, both with a neutral flavour, then add more flavouring to suit a particular dish.

Barbecue Oil for Meat

Place 1 × 5ml tsp (1tsp) coarsely chopped black peppercorns in a bottle with a wide neck. Add a couple of stems of lovage, and a sprig of thyme and parsley. Fill the bottle with oil and insert cork or use a screw top. Store in the fridge – it will be ready for use after 4–5 days. Pour the amount you are going to use into a small bowl and add onion, garlic, bay leaves, marjoram, basil, mustard, tomato purée etc.

Barbecue Oil for Fish

Place $\frac{1}{2}$ × 5ml tsp ($\frac{1}{2}$tsp) coarsely chopped white peppercorns, $\frac{1}{2}$ × 5ml tsp ($\frac{1}{2}$tsp) dried fennel or fennel seeds and a strip of lemon rind in a bottle with a wide neck. Add a couple of sprigs of parsley and 3–4 sprigs of thyme or dill. Fill bottle with oil, close tightly, and leave in the fridge for 4–5 days before use.

When you are going to use the oil, add onion, tomato purée, mustard, white wine vinegar etc.

Barbecue Sauces

These sauces are used to brush the food while grilling and as a sauce to accompany the grilled dish. There are many varieties in the shops, but they are not always tasty. Most of them have too much seasoning, have a penetrating vinegary flavour and are nearly always sweetened with sugar, which is quite unnecessary.
Here are some recipes for home-made sauces – they are very tasty and much more economical.

Sauce for Meat

Chop 4–5 small onions and sauté in 2–3 × 15ml tbsp (2–3tbsp) oil on not too strong heat, until golden. Stir in 1 × 15ml tbsp (1tbsp) flour and cook for a couple of minutes. Stir in 250ml (9fl oz) strong stock and about 200ml (7fl oz) red wine to make a smooth sauce. Boil for a few minutes. Season with salt, paprika, black pepper, a pinch of thyme, a dash of tomato purée and marjoram or basil. Keep warm.

Sauce for Fish

Finely chop 1 onion and sauté in 2 × 15ml tbsp (2tbsp) butter or oil on low heat. Add 250ml (9fl oz) fish stock (or water + cube) and simmer until onion is soft. Add 100–200ml (4–7fl oz) dry white wine and season with salt, lemon, pepper and a pinch of dried fennel.
What is left of the sauce after brushing can be thickened and served with the fish. Place saucepan in the centre of the barbecue grid and bring sauce to the boil. Dissolve 1–2 × 5ml tsp (1–2tsp) cornflour in cold water or white wine and add to saucepan while stirring vigorously. The sauce can also be thickened with 1 egg yolk mixed with 100ml (4fl oz) cream. Do not allow sauce to boil after adding the egg yolk.
Season with finely chopped dill or parsley.

Sauce for Poultry

Finely chop 2 small onions and sauté with ½–1 crushed garlic clove in 2–3 × 15ml tbsp (2–3tbsp) oil until onion is soft and transparent. Add 3–4 × 15ml tbsp (3–4tbsp) to-mato purée, 250ml (9fl oz) stock, 1 × 5ml tsp (1tsp) dried tarragon or basil. Bring to the boil and season with salt, pepper and paprika. Instead of tomato purée you can season with 1–2 × 5ml tsp (1–2tsp) light-coloured mustard and 1–2 × 15ml tbsp (1–2tbsp) lemon juice

Sauce for Vegetables

Slice or cut 5–6 thin slices of bacon into small strips or cubes and fry gently in a saucepan until fat es-capes. Add 2 × 15ml tbsp (2tbsp) oil, 2 finely chopped small onions, 1 crushed garlic clove, 1 grated carrot and/or ½ leek cut into thin rings. Sauté vegetables, stiring continu-ously and add 1 small can of to-matoes. Boil for 10–15 min until to-matoes are very soft, then add 100ml (4fl oz) white wine or light-coloured stock and 1 × 15ml tbsp (1tbsp) lemon juice. Bring sauce to the boil once more and season with salt, pepper, paprika and a little basil.

A homemade barbecue sauce makes good ingredients even tastier.

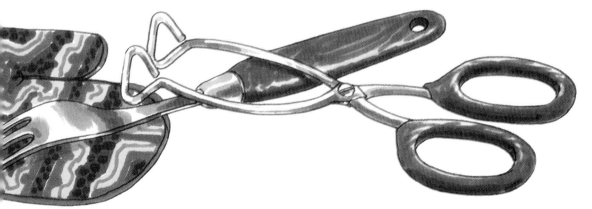

Savoury Butters and Cold Sauces

Salads, bread and baked potatoes are nearly always served with barbecued foods. The illustration above shows how you can serve the salad – everyone helps himself to the various vegetables and mixes his own.
Savoury butter and cold sauces add the little extra touch which makes the meal an experience of flavours.

Parsley Butter

Stir 100–125g (4–4½oz) softened butter with 4–5 × 15ml tbsp (4–5tbsp) chopped parsley and 1–2 × 5ml tsp (1–2tsp) lemon juice, and season with a little white pepper. You can also add 1 small grated onion and/or ½–1 crushed garlic clove. Shape butter into a roll, wrap in tinfoil and place in fridge. Cut into thick slices to serve. This butter is suitable for all kinds of meat, fish and vegetable dishes.

Dill, Chive and Tarragon Butters

Use same procedure as for Parsley Butter, but replace parsley with dill, chives or tarragon.

Paprika Butter

Stir 100–125g (4–4½oz) softened butter with 2–3 × 15ml tbsp (2–3tbsp) finely chopped red pepper, 1–2 × 5ml tsp (1–2tsp) lemon juice and 1–2 × 5ml tsp (1–2tsp) mild paprika. Serve with beef, poultry, smoked meats and offal.

Red Wine Butter

Stir 100–125g (4–4½oz) softened butter with 2–3 × 5ml tbsp (2–3tbsp) strong red wine, a little freshly ground black pepper, 1 grated shallot and ½–1 × 5ml tsp (½–1tsp) mild paprika. When butter roll is cold, roll in finely chopped parsley. Serve with beef and offal.

Cold Sauce (basic recipe)

Melt 25g (1oz) butter in a saucepan. Stir in 1½ × 15ml tbsp (1½tbsp) flour and sauté without browning for a couple of minutes. Stir in 300ml (½pt) light-coloured stock, or vegetable water and cream. Boil for 3–4 min. Cool, stirring from time to time. Carefully fold in 100ml (4fl oz) lightly whipped double cream and one of the following suggestions:

- chopped parsley, chives and/or other herbs, salt and white pepper.
- 100g (¼lb) sliced mushrooms sautéed in butter, salt and lemon juice.
- 1 finely chopped red or green pepper, salt, lemon juice.
- 2–3 × 15ml tbsp (2–3tbsp) tomato purée, 2 small grated onions, 1 crushed garlic clove, 2 × 15ml tbsp (2tbsp) finely chopped fresh basil and salt and pepper. Serve with all kinds of fish and vegetables.

Cheese Sauce

Mash 100g (¼lb) blue cheese until smooth. Add 8 × 15ml tbsp (8tbsp) oil, drop by drop. Mix in about 100ml (4fl oz) dry white wine, 1 × 5ml tsp (1tsp) lemon juice and a couple of drops of Worcestershire sauce. Serve with fish, poultry and vegetables.

Remoulade Sauce

To 300ml (½pt) homemade or bought mayonnaise, add 2 × 15ml tbsp (2tbsp) finely chopped cress, 1 × 5ml tsp (1tsp) Worcestershire sauce and 100ml (4fl oz) lightly whipped double cream. Serve with fish, sausages, smoked meats and patties.

A sliced savoury butter or a cold savoury sauce is just right for barbecued foods. Choose additional flavourings according to what you are grilling.

Cucumber Sauce

Mix 300ml (½pt) natural yoghurt with 1 × 5ml tsp (1tsp) lemon juice, 1–2 crushed garlic cloves, 3 × 15ml tbsp (3tbsp) small cubes of cucumber, and salt. Serve with beef, lamb, poultry and fish.

The Versatile Barbecue

Barbecued Trout

(serves 4)
Preparation time: 15 min
Cooking time: 10–15 min
Unsuitable for the freezer

4 × 250–300g (9–11oz) trout
salt, pepper
2 lemons
oil

1 Remove the heads, gut and wash fish, cut off fins. Sprinkle insides with a little salt and leave in a cool place for about 10 min. Dry fish inside and out with a soft cloth or paper towel and sprinkle insides with lemon juice.
2 Rub fish on the outside with salt and pepper and brush with oil. (The recipe for a special oil for fish, flavoured with lemon and herbs, is given on page 7.)
3 Place trout in a wire grill specially made for food which breaks up easily, or directly on grid, and cook about 10cm (4in) away from embers. Turn often and brush with oil a couple of times when fish starts to brown.
Serve with bread, Dill Butter (see page 10) and lemon wedges.

Smoked Fish

This method of cooking is particularly suitable for trout, herring and small mackerel, but any fish must be salted before smoking.
There are many kinds of smoke cooker available, all of which come complete with manufacturer's instructions, but you can just as easily use a large iron casserole placed on the grid. Smoking is best undertaken outdoors to avoid the smell of smoke permeating the house.
Place a layer of sawdust or fine wood shavings at the bottom of the casserole, and cover with a 10–15cm (4–6in) thick layer mixed with a few dried fennel stems and juniper twigs. Place casserole on fairly strong heat until it starts smoking, meanwhile salt fish and sprinkle insides with a little lemon juice.
Place fish on a grid in the casserole. Cover with a damp cloth and then

with a tight-fitting lid. Place something heavy on lid and leave casserole on heat as close to embers as possible for 10 min. Raise grid and casserole to about 10–15 cm (4–6in) from embers, and smoke trout and mackerel for a further 10–15 min. Herring needs only 10 min in the smoke. Serve hot with bread, butter and lemon wedges.

Pork Schnitzels on Skewers

(serves 4)
Preparation time: 15 min
Cooking time: 15–20 min
Suitable for the freezer, but will lose some flavour

4 fairly thick slices pork fillet
    (tenderloin)
4–5 × 15ml tbsp (4–5tbsp) oil
1 × 5ml tsp (1tsp) dried mixed herbs
1 pinch of cayenne
¼ × 5ml tsp (¼tsp) black pepper
salt

1 Beat meat slices until flattened and thin. Blend oil with mixed herbs, cayenne pepper and coarsely ground black pepper, and brush meat slices on both side.
2 Fold meat slices double and thread onto skewers or thin twigs without bark. Cook on grid 10–15cm (4–6in) away from embers, turning often and brushing with the flavoured oil. Sprinkle with salt when meat is brown.
Serve warm with bread or baked potatoes, a herb butter and a green salad.

Eggs with Onion and Bacon

(serves 4)
Preparation time: 15 min
Cooking time: 6–8 min
Unsuitable for the freezer

8 thin slices of bacon
1 large onion
4 eggs
salt, pepper
finely chopped parsley

1 Cut bacon into small pieces, and divide between 4 small dishes made from double tinfoil.
2 Put dishes on barbecue grid about 10cm (4in) away from embers, until bacon fat starts to melt. Coarsely chop the onion, mix with bacon and cook for a further 2–3 min.
3 Break one egg at a time into a

cup and slide carefully into a dish. When egg white is cooked, sprinkle with salt, pepper and finely chopped parsley.
Serve as a starter or as an individual dish with bread and butter. A green salad goes well with these eggs.

Spare Rib Barbecue

(serves 4)
Preparation time: 10 min
Marinating time: 2 hr
Cooking time: about 30 min
Suitable for the freezer

1½kg (3lb) piece of spare rib
oil
salt
Marinade:
1 onion
1 × 15ml tbsp (1tbsp) wine vinegar
1 × 5ml tsp (1tsp) Worcestershire
    sauce
100ml (4fl oz) red wine
2 × 15ml tbsp (2tbsp) tomato purée
1 × 5ml tsp (1tsp) paprika
½ × 5ml tsp (½tsp) curry powder
¼ × 5ml tsp (¼tsp) pepper
½ × 5ml tsp (½tsp) ground ginger
1 × 5ml tsp (1tsp) dried herbs

1 Cut away most of the fat from the pork and divide the joint into 4 pieces, each with 2–3 ribs. Place in a deep dish.
2 Mix together marinade of grated onion and other ingredients. Pour over meat and leave in a cool place, turning several times, for 2 hr.
3 Wipe marinade off meat pieces, brush with oil, and place on grid. This should be about 15 cm (6in) away from embers.
Turn meat often and brush with marinade mixed with a little oil. When meat is quite tender, sprinkle over a little salt. Serve with a French loaf and remaining marinade or with baked potatoes and Red Wine Butter or Paprika Butter. Also serve a simple salad.

Almost anything can be barbecued – even fried eggs! Pictured here are fish, pork schnitzels, spare ribs, and fried eggs on top of bacon in small tinfoil dishes.

Juicy Steaks with Trimmings

Steaks with Herb Butter

(below)
(serves 4)
Preparation time: 20 min
Marinating time: 2 hr
Cooking time: about 6 min
Unsuitable for the freezer

4 thick entrecôte steaks
salt, pepper
oil
4 tomatoes
Marinade :
4–5 × 15ml tbsp (4–5tbsp) oil
1 × 5ml tsp (1tsp) strong made
  mustard
½ × 5ml tsp (½tsp) black pepper
1 × 5ml tsp (1tsp) dried, crushed
  thyme and rosemary or 1 crushed
  garlic clove
Herb butter :
100g (4oz) softened butter
½–1 crushed garlic clove

pinch of white pepper
4 × 15ml tbsp (4tbsp) fresh, finely
  chopped green herbs (parsley, sage,
  tarragon, thyme, basil)

1 Beat steaks lightly with your hand.
2 Mix marinade, sprinkle over steaks, and place them in a cold place, turning from time to time.
3 Mix together all the herb butter ingredients. Shape butter into a roll on a piece of tinfoil, wrap and put in a cool place.
4 Wipe marinade off steaks and fry for 2–3 min each side with the barbecue grid near the embers. If you want the steaks to be well done, move grid a little further from embers and fry ½–2 min longer each side. Season cooked steaks with salt.
5 Wash tomatoes, cut in half, and season cut edge with salt and pepper. Brush with a little oil or marinade and fry on barbecue grid, near embers, for 2–4 min.
Serve steaks hot with a slice of herb butter on top of each, and with the fried tomatoes and a salad.

Entrecôte Steaks with Tomatoes (right)
(serves 4)
Preparation time: 15 min
Cooking time: 4–6 min
Unsuitable for the freezer

4 × 200g (7oz) thick entrecôte
steaks, preferably with outside fat
salt, black pepper
oil or Barbecue Oil (see page 7)
8 tomatoes

1 Beat meat lightly with the back of your hand. Rub with black pepper and brush with a little oil. If using Barbecue Oil, omit the pepper. Leave meat in a cool place.
2 Cut a cross in the tomatoes, sprinkle this with salt, and brush tomatoes with oil. Wrap each tomato in strong tinfoil and place along the outer edge of barbecue grid. Turn from time to time.
3 Place steaks in centre of grid, about 8cm (3in) from embers. Grill for 2–3 min each side and season with salt.
Serve hot with tomatoes, baked potatoes, Red Wine Butter (see page 10), and a simple green salad.

Potatoes Baked in Tinfoil
(serves 4)
Preparation time: 3 min
Cooking time: 1–1½ hr
Unsuitable for the freezer

8 medium-sized potatoes
1 × 15ml tbsp (1tbsp) oil
salt

1 Scrub potatoes well and dry thoroughly. Prick with a barbecue skewer or fork to prevent them bursting while cooking.
2 Brush with a little oil and wrap in strong tinfoil. Place on grid, and turn often while cooking. Insert a thin needle to see if potatoes are tender.
3 Open tinfoil carefully and fold back. Make an incision in the potatoes, sprinkle this with salt, and serve with herb butter.

Potatoes Baked in Ashes
When there is about 5cm (2in) of ash at the bottom of the barbecue from previous grillings, don't empty the ashes.
Place fresh pieces of charcoal or briquettes on top and set alight. Mix ashes well with the new glowing

coals and pull them towards the side. Bury potatoes, wrapped in tinfoil, in this, making sure you have ashes and embers all round them. After about ½ hr, place more coal in the middle of the barbecue. When these coals are white hot, and potatoes have been buried for 1 hr, place meat or fish on the grid.
Remove foil from the potatoes, and wrap in fresh foil with the opening facing up so that you can make an incision in each potato. Season this with salt, and put a dollop of herb butter on top.

Pepper Steaks with Cream Sauce
(serves 4)
Preparation time: 10 min
Marinating time: about 1 hr
Cooking time: 4–6 min
Unsuitable for the freezer

4 × 175g (6oz) entrecôte steaks
1 × 15ml tbsp (1tbsp) soft, green
* peppercorns*
about 200–300ml (7–10fl oz) double
* cream or sour cream*
1–2 × 5ml tsp (1–2tsp)
* Worcestershire sauce*
1 onion
oil
salt

1 Beat steaks lightly with the back of your hand and rub with about ½ × 15ml tbsp (½tbsp) mashed, soft peppercorns. Place steaks on a dish and pour over lightly whipped double cream or sour cream, mixed with Worcestershire sauce and finely grated onion. Leave in a cool place, covered, for about 1 hr.
2 Wipe marinade off steaks, and brush them with oil. Grill for 2–3 min each side, about 8–10cm

(3–4in) away from the embers.
Season with salt.
3 Stir the remaining peppercorns
into sour cream or lightly whipped
cream mixture and season with salt.
The peppercorns give the sauce a
strong flavour. Stir in more cream or
sour cream if necessary.
Serve steaks with the cream sauce,
baked potatoes and a salad.

Rosemary Steaks

(serves 4)
Preparation time: 15 min
Marinating time: about 12 hr
Cooking time: 5–8 min
Unsuitable for the freezer

4 × 175g (6oz) entrecôte steaks
oil
fresh or dried rosemary
1 clove garlic
salt, black pepper
4 tomatoes

1 Beat steaks lightly with the back
of your hand and rub with oil.
Firmly press fresh rosemary leaves
onto each side of the steaks, or rub
with a little crushed dried rosemary.
Place steaks on top of each other and
leave in the fridge overnight.
2 Wipe off rosemary and rub steaks
with crushed garlic and about
$\frac{1}{2}$ × 5ml tsp ($\frac{1}{2}$tsp) black pepper.
Make cuts in tomatoes at the top,
season with salt, and brush with oil.
3 Grill steaks and tomatoes on grid
10–15cm (4–6in) away from embers.
The steaks should be cooked for
2–4 min each side, depending on
how well done you want them.
The tomatoes should be cooked for
4–5 min. Serve with Paprika Butter
(see page 10) and a French loaf,
or with baked potatoes or a cold
potato salad. Sprinkle a few fresh
rosemary leaves over both tomatoes
and steaks.

Minute Steaks

(serves 4)
Preparation time: 15 min
Cooking time: 6–8 min
Unsuitable for the freezer

2 aubergines (egg plants)
salt, black pepper
8 thin entrecôte or rump steaks
oil
1 sprig watercress or a little ordinary
  cress

1 Wash and slice aubergines.
Sprinkle with salt and leave in a
colander, under light pressure, for
about 10 min.
2 Beat meat with your hand until
thin. Never use a meat basher, as
this destroys the fibres and makes
the meat dry. Rub with a little black
pepper.
3 Dry aubergine slices and meat
with paper towels and brush with

oil. Place aubergine slices on a wire on the barbecue and cook for about 2 min each side, about 8–10cm (3–4in) away from the coals.

4 Move aubergine slices to the outer edge of the grid and grill the thin steaks for ½–1 min each side. Sprinkle with salt after browning. Place steaks on top of aubergine slices and garnish with cress or watercress.

Serve with a mixed green salad and sliced boiled potatoes.

Farmer's Steak

(serves 6)
Preparation time: 2–3 min
Cooking time: 6–8 min
Unsuitable for the freezer

6 × 175–200g (6–7oz) entrecôte or
  rump steaks with outside fat
salt, pepper
oil

1 Make two or three small snicks in the fat, and rub meat with coarsely ground pepper.

2 Brush steaks with oil or Barbecue Oil (see page 7). If the latter, omit pepper. Grill for 3–4 min each side about 10cm (4in) away from embers. Season with salt.

Serve with grilled tomatoes or other vegetables, bread or rolls and Celeriac and Apple Salad.

Celeriac and Apple Salad

(serves 6)
Preparation time: 15 min
Unsuitable for the freezer

½ celeriac
2–3 sharp apples
juice of 1 lemon
100ml (4fl oz) mayonnaise
100ml (4fl oz) double cream
salt
cayenne

Left: Rosemary Steaks.
Above: Farmer's Steak with Celeriac and Apple Salad.

1 Peel celeriac, peel and core apples, and coarsely grate both. Squeeze lemon juice over to avoid discoloration.

2 Blend mayonnaise with lightly whipped cream and mix in celeriac and apple. Season with salt and a pinch of cayenne.

Serve chilled.

VARIATION

Use 2–3 stalks of finely cut celery instead of celeriac. They are equally tasty and usually considerably cheaper.

Beef Rib and T-Bone Steaks

Châteaubriand
(Porterhouse Steak)
(serves 2–3)
Preparation time: 15 min
Cooking time: about 20 min
Unsuitable for the freezer

1 slice of fillet steak (tenderloin),
  5–6cm (2–2½in) thick
1 × 15ml tbsp (1tbsp) red wine
3 × 15ml tbsp (3tbsp) oil
black pepper, salt
200g (7oz) shallots
6 small tomatoes
cress

1 Make small incisions in the fatty edge and rub meat with coarsely ground black pepper. Brush with red wine and oil whisked lightly together. Leave in a cool place for about 10 min.
2 Scald and peel shallots. Boil for about 5 min in lightly salted water and drain through a colander.
Make a criss-cross cut in tomatoes and sprinkle with salt.
3 Grill meat for about 5 min each side on good heat. Then move barbecue grid until it is about 15cm (6in) away from embers, or cover

Serve Wing Ribs with Red Wine Butter and Grilled Tomatoes. T-bone Steaks with Béarnaise Sauce.

these with ashes if grid is non-adjustable.
4 Brush shallots and tomatoes with red wine and oil, and place on grid. Brush meat with oil while it rests on grid, loosely covered, for 5–10 min before being cut into slices at an angle. Serve with lightly grilled onion and tomatoes. Garnish with cress and accompany with a French loaf, or with baked potatoes with Paprika Butter or Parsley Butter (see page 10).

Wing Ribs or T-Bone Steaks

(Côtes de Boeuf)
(serves 4)
Preparation time: 15 min
Marinating time: about 1 hr
Cooking time: 6–8 min
Unsuitable for the freezer

4 wing ribs or T-bone steaks, about 2cm (¾in) thick
4 × 15ml tbsp (4tbsp) Red Wine Marinade (see pages 6, 41)
oil
salt
watercress or ordinary cress

1 Make a couple of incisions in the fatty edge of the chops and beat them lightly with your hand. Brush with Red Wine Marinade and leave in a cool place for about 1 hr.
2 Dry chops lightly with paper towels, brush with oil and grill for 3–4 min each side, fairly close to the charcoal. Season with salt.
Serve hot, garnished with cress. A French loaf, Red Wine Butter (see page 10) and grilled tomatoes go well with this dish.

Grilled Tomatoes

Wash tomatoes, cut in half and sprinkle with salt, pepper and a little finely chopped or crushed, dried basil. Sprinkle with oil and grill, flat side up, for 2 min at the side of the barbecue grid. Turn, place nearer centre of grid and grill for 2–3 min more.

T-Bone Steaks with Garlic Potatoes

(serves 4)
Preparation time: 15 min
Cooking, potatoes: about 45 min
Cooking meat: 6–8 min
Unsuitable for the freezer

4 T-bone steaks, about 2cm (¾in) thick
1 quantity Barbecue Oil with garlic (see page 7)
salt, black pepper
4–6 medium-sized potatoes
1–2 cloves garlic

1 Brush meat with the oil, and leave in a cool place until potatoes are nearly done.
2 Scrub potatoes and dry well. Cut in half lengthways and rub the cut sides with crushed garlic, salt and pepper. Brush with oil and place along the edge of barbecue grid. Turn several times, and brush from time to time with oil.
3 Sprinkle a little coarsely ground pepper onto steaks and grill for 3–4 min each side, 8–10cm (3–4in) away from the embers. Serve with potatoes and chilled butter or Béarnaise Sauce.

Béarnaise Sauce

150g (5oz) butter
4 egg yolks
100ml (4fl oz) meat or chicken stock
2 × 15ml tbsp (2tbsp) Béarnaise essence (see note)
salt, white pepper
1 × 15ml tbsp (1tbsp) finely chopped, mixed chervil and parsley

1 Slice butter into a thick-bottomed saucepan. (Do not use aluminium, as this might discolour sauce.)
2 Add egg yolks, stock and essence. Place saucepan on very low heat and stir constantly until sauce is smooth and thick. Do not boil, or sauce will curdle.
3 Season with salt and pepper and stir in herbs. Keep sauce warm over a saucepan of hot, but not boiling, water.
NOTE If the sauce curdles, you can save it by whisking in an ice cube or a couple of spoonfuls of ice-cold water. If you cannot obtain this essence put 2 × 15ml tbsp (2tbsp) each of dry white wine and tarragon vinegar into a pan. Add 1 small finely chopped onion and a small sprig of finely chopped parsley. Boil until only half liquid remains, then strain.

A Touch of Luxury

Tournedos

(serves 4)
Preparation time: 10 min
Cooking time: 6–8 min
Unsuitable for the freezer

4 tournedos (cut from fillet) 3–4cm
  (1¼–1½in) thick
4 slices rindless pork
black pepper
oil
salt

1 Beat steaks lightly with your
hand, then shape into thick rounds.
Rub with pepper and brush with oil.
2 Sprinkle one side of pork slices
with salt and pepper. Place around
steaks, seasoned side inwards, and
fasten with skewers.
3 Lift one steak at a time with barbecue tongs and hold with the pork
edge facing the barbecue grid. Turn
round until nice and brown, then
place steak on grid and cook for
2–3 min each side. Season with salt.

Tournedos with Special Stuffing (above)

(serves 4)
Preparation time: 15–20 min
Cooking time: 6–8 min
Unsuitable for the freezer

8 thin slices tenderloin or 4 thick
  slices entrecôte steaks
2 × 15ml tbsp (2tbsp) soft blue cheese
4 × 15ml tbsp (4tbsp) finely chopped
  parsley
dill, chives or cress
oil
salt, pepper
4 slices rindless pork or bacon

1 Beat meat slices lightly with your
hand and rub with pepper. Slice
thick fillets across. Mash cheese
with a fork, mix with herbs and a
little oil and stir until smooth.
2 Divide cheese mixture between 4
slices of beef and place the other 4
slices on top. Squeeze edges tightly
together and place pork or bacon
around. Fasten with skewers or
toothpicks. Cook as for Tournedos
(left).
Serve with butter or herb butter,
and a tomato salad.

Veal Cordon Bleu

(serves 4)
Preparation time: 20 min
Cooking time: 15–20 min
Suitable for the freezer, but will lose
some flavour

4 large, thin slices of veal
4 slices cooked ham
4 slices cheese
1 sprig of thyme or 1 bay leaf
Barbecue Oil (see page 7)
salt, pepper

1 Beat meat slices lightly with your
hand. Season with a little pepper
and place ham and cheese on top.
Place a few fresh thyme leaves or a
finely chopped bay leaf over, and
roll up meat slices firmly. Fasten
with thread or skewers.
2 Brush rolls with lightly seasoned
oil, and cook on grid 12–15cm
(5–6in) away from embers, turning
often and brushing from time to
time with a little oil.
Serve with bread and a tomato salad,
or with a mixed green salad containing slices of boiled potato.

Right : Veal Cordon Bleu

Minced Meat
Favourites

**Minced Meat Rolls with
Vegetables** (left)
(serves 4)
Preparation time: 15–20 min
Cooking time: 10–12 min
Suitable for the freezer, without
vegetables

½kg (1lb 2oz) minced beef, mixed
   with a little minced pork
1–2 cloves garlic
2–3 shallots
2 × 15ml tbsp (2tbsp) oil
salt, black pepper
paprika
sage
tarragon
marjoram
4 courgettes
4–6 tomatoes
oil for brushing
parsley

1 Rinse and dry courgettes and tomatoes. Cut courgettes lengthways,
season with salt, and put in a cool
place for 10–15 min.
2 Meanwhile mix minced meat with
crushed garlic, finely chopped shallots, oil, seasonings and fresh or
dried herbs Allow mixture to settle
for 10–15 min.
3 Shape into 8 rolls and brush with
oil. Rinse salt from courgettes,
brush with oil, and grill with meat
rolls on grid about 15cm (6in) away
from embers for 10–12 min, turning
often. Halve tomatoes, season flat
side and brush it with oil. Place on
grid flat side down, for the last
2–3 min of cooking time.
Sprinkle finely chopped parsley over
vegetables. Serve with brown bread
or rolls, Parsley Butter with garlic
(see page 10), and a simple green
salad.

VARIATION
The minced beef can be mixed with capers, crushed garlic, grated horse-radish, soft green peppercorns, chopped pickled gherkins or pickled pearl onions. Instead of salt and pepper, mix in herbs.

Serving Suggestion
Beefburgers can be served with fried onion, fried bacon, raw cucumber slices or cucumber salad, pickles or small gherkins. You can also place fried egg, sliced hardboiled egg or raw egg yolk on top. Pour a little tomato purée, Worcestershire sauce, or mayonnaise seasoned with salt, pepper and paprika, over burgers before serving.

Barbecued Meatballs
(serves 5–6)
Preparation time: 15 min
Settling time: about 30 min
Cooking time: 10–15 min
Suitable for the freezer

Beefburgers
(serves 6)
Preparation time: 10 min
Cooking time: 2–4 min
Suitable for the freezer, but will lose some flavour

750g (1lb 10oz) minced beef
1 egg
3 onions
black pepper, salt
oil
3 tomatoes
6 baps

1 Mix minced beef with egg, 1 finely chopped onion and $\frac{1}{2} \times$ 5ml tsp ($\frac{1}{2}$tsp) coarsely ground black pepper.

Divide and shape into 6 large, flat patties.
2 Wash tomatoes, cut into thick slices and sprinkle with salt and pepper. Peel remaining 2 onions and cut into thin rings or coarsely chop.
3 Brush beefburgers with oil and fry for 1–2 min each side, 6–8cm ($2\frac{1}{2}$–3in) away from embers.
Sprinkle tomato slices with oil and warm at the outer edge of barbecue grid. Sprinkle a little salt onto cooked patties.
4 Cut baps in half and place beef-burgers, tomato slices, raw onion rings or chopped onion inside. Serve hot with a little mustard and ketchup.

½kg (1lb 2oz) minced beef
250g (9oz) pork sausagemeat
3 × 15ml tbsp (3tbsp) breadcrumbs
4 × 15ml tbsp (4tbsp) cream
1 clove garlic and/or 2–3 shallots
salt, pepper
paprika
50–75g (2–3oz) butter
chives, oil

1 Thoroughly mix together minced beef, sausagemeat, breadcrumbs, cream, crushed garlic and/or finely chopped shallots and seasonings.
2 Slice chilled butter and mix with finely chopped chives and a little paprika, softening butter as little as possible.

3 Divide meat mixture into large meat balls. Push a little savoury butter into the centre of each ball and squeeze opening together. Place balls on a dish, brush with a little oil, and leave in a cool place, covered, for about $\frac{1}{2}$ hr.

4 Brush barbecue grid, 12–15cm (5–6in) away from embers, with a little oil. Place balls on grid and cook, turning often, until brown.

Minced Beef Patties with Herbs

(serves 4)
Preparation time: 15 min
Cooking time: 6–8 min
Suitable for the freezer, but will lose some flavour

750g (1lb 10oz) minced beef or minced beef with a little minced pork
1 egg
black pepper, salt
2 shallots
3 × 15ml tbsp (3tbsp) finely chopped herbs (eg fennel, parsley or chervil)
oil, paprika

1 Pound minced meat with $\frac{1}{2}$ × 5ml tsp ($\frac{1}{2}$tsp) salt until it feels very firm. Add lightly whisked egg, $\frac{1}{4}$ × 5ml tsp ($\frac{1}{4}$tsp) pepper, finely chopped shallots, paprika to taste and herbs. Divide and shape to form 8 flat patties.

2 Brush patties with oil and cook for 3–4 min each side on a hot grid. Sprinkle with salt when cooked.

VARIATION
Minced Beef Patties are even tastier with a fried egg on top.

Spanish Potato Salad

(serves 4)
Preparation time: 15 min
Unsuitable for the freezer

6–8 boiled potatoes
2 shallots
3 ripe tomatoes
1 green pepper
chives
2 × 15ml tbsp (2tbsp) lemon juice
salt, pepper
4–5 × 15ml tbsp (4–5tbsp) olive oil

1 Slice potatoes into a bowl, and mix in finely chopped shallots, Blend together a marinade of salt, pepper, lemon juice and olive oil, and sprinkle one half over potatoes and onion.

2 Wash tomatoes and pepper. Slice tomatoes, cut pepper into thin rings.

3 Place tomatoes and pepper in layers over potatoes, sprinkle over chopped chives and remaining marinade. Make this salad well in advance, and leave in a cool place for a while so that flavours can blend, before serving.

Left: Barbecued Meatballs.
Above: Minced Beef Patties with Herbs and Spanish Potato Salad.

Tasty Sausages

Sausages and Garlic Bread on Skewers

(serves 4)
Preparation time: 10 min
Cooking time: 6–8 min
Unsuitable for the freezer

8 barbecue sausages
4 thick slices of bread
3–4 × 15ml tbsp (3–4tbsp) oil
1 clove garlic
salt, pepper
paprika
4 ripe tomatoes
watercress or lettuce
juice of ½ lemon

1 Slice each sausage into four, and bread slices into cubes of about the same size. Thread pieces of sausage and bread onto skewers.
2 Mix oil with crushed garlic, ½ × 5ml tsp (½tsp) salt, ¼ × 5ml tsp (¼tsp) black pepper and ½ × 5ml tsp (½tsp) paprika. Brush sausages and bread with oil and place skewers on barbecue about 10cm (4in) away from embers. Cook until brown, turning often and brushing several times with oil.

3 Place the hot skewers on a bed of fresh watercress or lettuce leaves and tomato wedges. Sprinkle skewers with lemon juice, and tomatoes with salt and pepper.
Strong, unsweetened mustard is the only accompaniment necessary.

Stuffed Sausages

(serves 4)
Preparation time: 10–15 min
Cooking time: 5–6 min
Unsuitable for the freezer

8 barbecue sausages
1 × 15ml tbsp (1tbsp) made mustard
1 onion
1 × 15ml tbsp (1tbsp) soy sauce
1 × 15ml tbsp (1tbsp) tomato purée
8 slices of bacon

1 Make a deep incision lengthways in the sausages. Mix mustard with finely grated or chopped onion, soy sauce and tomato purée, and insert in the incisions.
2 Press sausages carefully together and wrap a slice of bacon around them. Fasten with toothpicks or skewers. Cook on barbecue grid,

Left: Sausages and Garlic Bread on Skewers.
Above: Sausages with Skewered Potatoes.

8–10cm (3–4in) away from embers. Turn often and move grid higher up if the bacon becomes too brown.

VARIATION

Spread a thin layer of mustard in the incisions and insert thick strips of firm, mild cheese. Tie bacon slices around, or close the openings with skewers if you don't use bacon. Grill sausages on one side only, otherwise the cheese will ooze out.

Sausages with Skewered Potatoes

(serves 4)
Preparation time: 15 min
Marinating time: about 30 min
Cooking time: 25–30 min

8 barbecue sausages
½–¾kg (about 1½lb) potatoes
4–5 × 15ml tbsp (4–5tbsp) olive oil
2 × 15ml tbsp (2tbsp) lemon juice
salt, pepper
sage, oil for brushing

1 Peel potatoes and cut into fairly thick slices or pieces – large ones are

first cut lengthways. Mix a marinade of oil, lemon juice, 1 × 5ml tsp (1tsp) salt, ¼ × 5ml tsp (¼tsp) pepper and ½ × 15ml tbsp (½tbsp) finely chopped fresh, or ½ × 5ml tsp (½tsp) dried, sage leaves. Pour marinade over potatoes, and turn them occasionally.
2 Thread potatoes onto skewers and place on grid 12–15cm (5–6in) away from embers. Turn skewers often, and brush with oil to prevent potatoes sticking to the grid.
3 When potatoes are nearly cooked, move skewers towards the edge of barbecue grid and place the sausages in the middle. Brush with a little oil, and grill for 2–3 min each side.

Lamb Chops and Kebabs

Lamb Chops with Bean Purée
(above)
(serves 4–6)
Preparation time: 15–20 min
Cooking time: about 15 min
Unsuitable for the freezer

8–12 single, or 4–6 double, lamb
   chops (see picture page 58)
1 clove garlic
salt, pepper
rosemary
thyme
oil
½kg (1lb 2oz) runner beans
100ml (4fl oz) double cream
grated nutmeg
chopped parsley

1 Rinse and string beans, cut large
ones in half. Boil in lightly salted
water, drain, and steam until dry.

2 Rub chops with crushed garlic,
½ × 5ml tsp (½tsp) pepper and a little
fresh or dried rosemary and thyme.
3 Run beans through a blender
until you have a smooth purée.
Whisk in cream, season with salt,
pepper and nutmeg, and keep warm.
4 Brush chops with oil, and cook on
grid about 10cm (4in) away from
embers. Sprinkle purée with chopped parsley.
Serve with grilled tomatoes, foil-
baked potatoes and Parsley Butter
(see page 10).

Lamb Kebabs
(serves 4–6)
Preparation time: 20 min
Marinating time: about 2 hr
Cooking time: 12–15 min
Unsuitable for the freezer

½–¾kg (about 1½lb) tender lamb
8 shallots
8 small tomatoes
1–2 green peppers
4 bay leaves

salt
Marinade:
1 lemon
100–150ml (4–5fl oz) olive oil
pepper, marjoram
rosemary, basil

1 Cut meat into even-sized, fairly
large cubes and place in a dish. Mix
together a marinade of finely grated
lemon rind, lemon juice, ½ × 5ml tsp
(½tsp) coarsely ground pepper and
2 × 15ml tbsp (2tbsp) fresh, or 2 ×
5ml tsp (2tsp) dried, finely crushed
herbs. Pour marinade over meat and
put, covered, in a cool place.
2 Scald and peel shallots. Rinse tomatoes, rinse and deseed peppers
and cut into broad strips. Cut bay
leaves into two.
3 Thread meat, shallots, tomatoes,
pepper and bay leaves onto skewers,
brush with marinade and fry on barbecue grid 10–12cm (4–5in) away
from embers. Turn skewers often,
and brush with more marinade and
season with salt when cooked.

Lamb Chops with Peppers

(below)
(serves 4–6)
Preparation time: 10–15 min
Cooking time: 8–10 min
Unsuitable for the freezer

8–12 lamb chops
1 clove garlic
oil
salt, pepper
paprika
rosemary
marjoram
2–3 green or red peppers

1 Rub and brush lamb chops with crushed garlic, oil, seasonings and fresh or dried herbs.
2 Rinse and dry peppers. Hold over barbecue one at a time and turn until they are burnt on all sides. Skin, cut in half, remove all seeds and brush well with oil.
3 Place chops and halved peppers on the grid and cook for 4–5 min each side, 10–12cm (4–5in) from embers. Turn frequently. Serve with brown bread and Greek Feta Salad.

Greek Feta Salad

(serves 4–6)
Preparation time: 15 min
Unsuitable for the freezer

5–6 ripe tomatoes
½ cucumber
1–2 onions
200g (7oz) feta cheese (or cottage cheese)
50g (2oz) black olives
4 × 15ml tbsp (4tbsp) finely chopped parsley
1 × 15ml tbsp (1tbsp) fresh, or ½–1 × 5ml tsp (½–1tsp) dried, oregano
2 × 15ml tbsp (2tbsp) wine vinegar
salt, pepper
5–6 × 15ml tbsp (5–6tbsp) olive oil

1 Rinse tomatoes and cucumber, cut into slices. Peel onions and cut into thin rings. Mix together in a wide, but not too deep, dish.
2 Cut cheese into cubes and arrange over vegetables with well-drained olives. Mix parsley with remaining ingredients and sprinkle over salad. The salad can be prepared and put in a cool place about ½ hr before serving.

Barbecued Leg of Lamb barded with
juniper berries and served with
marinated French Beans.

Saddle of Lamb Barded with Herbs

(serves 5–6)
Preparation time: 20 min
Cooking time: about 1 hr
Suitable for the freezer, but will lose
some flavour

1 saddle of lamb
2–3 cloves garlic
2 sprigs of mint
1 sprig of thyme
2 sprigs of parsley
4–5 × 15ml tbsp (4–5tbsp) oil
juice of 1 lemon
salt, black pepper
lemon pepper (optional)
white wine
200–300ml (7–10fl oz) sour cream

1 Wipe saddle of lamb well with a
damp cloth and cut 12–15 small
incisions in it with a small sharp
knife (see illustrations, page 31).
2 Rinse herbs and pick off leaves.
Cut garlic into small slivers. Insert
garlic, thyme and most of mint and
parsley into incisions with a knife.
Fresh herbs can be replaced by
dried ones. Use 1 × 5ml tsp (1tsp)
mint and $\frac{1}{4}$–$\frac{1}{2}$ × 5ml tsp ($\frac{1}{4}$–$\frac{1}{2}$tsp)
thyme mixed with coarsely chopped
parsley.
3 Insert one or two barbecue
skewers into saddle to make it stiff
and keep it balanced. Insert the rotating spit, the claws in both ends of
roast.
4 Place lamb as far away from
embers as possible. Put a tray folded
from double tinfoil directly underneath meat and bank charcoal
around tray. Make sure the heat is
even. Brush meat with a mixture of
oil and lemon juice, and sprinkle
with salt, pepper and lemon pepper several times during roasting.
Lemon pepper goes very well with
lamb.
5 Cooking time varies, depending
on thickness of meat and heat of the
barbecue. Test by inserting a skewer
into the thicket part of the meat. The
juices escaping should be pink, so
that the meat is still faintly rare
inside. Remove meat from spit,
place, loosely covered, on a bread-

Saddle and Leg of lamb

*A juicy roast, barded with garlic and herbs and deliciously crisp
on the outside, is just the thing for a large barbecue party.*

board, and leave for 15 min to settle before carving.

Deglaze tinfoil tray with a little white wine and the sour cream. Season, and add freshly chopped parsley and mint. Serve lamb with bread and tomatoes or other vegetables which are grilled while meat is resting.

Barbecued Leg of Lamb

(serves 5–6)
Preparation time: 20 min
Resting time: 3–4 hr
Cooking time: 1¼–1½ hr
Suitable for the freezer, but will lose some flavour

1 leg of lamb (about 2kg [4½lb])
200g (7oz) rindless fat
10–12 dried juniper berries
1 × 5ml tsp (1tsp) paprika
½ × 5ml tsp (½tsp) pepper
100ml (4fl oz) oil
100ml (4fl oz) red wine or stock
1 × 5ml tsp (1tsp) Worcestershire
* sauce*
juice of ½ lemon
salt

1 Wipe leg of mutton well with a damp cloth and rub with paprika and pepper. Make small cuts about 2cm (¾in) deep with a pointed knife (see illustrations).
2 Leave fat in a cool place until you are ready to use it. Cut into small, thick strips. Insert juniper berries and fat into the cuts, wrap meat loosely, and leave in the fridge for 3–4 hr.
3 Place leg of mutton on rotating spit and attach to the barbecue, as far away from the embers as possible. Fold a tray of double tinfoil and place under roast to catch escaping juices. Mix oil, red wine, Worcestershire sauce and lemon juice, and brush lamb often with this mixture. Sprinkle with salt when lightly brown.
4 Cooking time depends on thickness of the meat and on the heat from the barbecue. Insert a skewer into the thickest part of the leg to see if it is ready. If the meat juices are pink, the meat done; if the juices are red, the meat should be cooked for another 15–20 min.
5 Place meat on a breadboard and leave for 15–20 min before carving. Deglaze the tinfoil tray with a little stock or red wine, and serve sauce

with meat along with baked potatoes and Marinated French Beans (below).

NOTE It is because larger joints contain so much juice which tends to escape, that you have to make a tinfoil tray to collect it. Place tray directly underneath meat and bank the charcoal around.

Marinated French Beans

(serves 5–6)
Preparation time: 15 min
Marinating time: at least 2 hr
Cooking time: 8–10 min
Unsuitable for the freezer

½–¾kg (about 1½lb) French beans
Marinade:
1 × 15ml tbsp (1tbsp) wine vinegar
1 × 15ml tbsp (1tbsp) lemon juice
½ × 5ml tsp (½tsp) salt
¼ × 5ml tsp (¼tsp) pepper
6 × 15ml tbsp (6tbsp) oil
2 shallots
1 clove garlic
3–4 × 15ml tbsp (3–4tbsp) finely
* chopped parsley*

1 Wash and slice beans. Boil until tender in lightly salted water and drain well.
2 Shake together a marinade of vinegar, lemon juice, salt, pepper, oil, finely chopped shallots, crushed garlic and parsley.
3 Pour marinade over beans and leave in a cool place, turning beans from time to time.

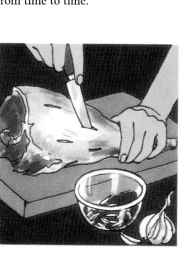

Barding a Leg of Lamb

1 Wipe leg of lamb well and make 12–15 small, 2cm (¾in) deep, incisions in it with a pointed knife.

2 Cut garlic into small slivers and insert these and herbs or other ingredients into incisions.

31

Barbecued Pork

Californian Chops (below)
(serves 4)
Preparation time: 10–15 min
Cooking time: about 8 min
Unsuitable for the freezer

4 large chops
oil
salt, pepper
3 × 15ml tbsp (3tbsp) apple juice
1 × 15ml tbsp (1tbsp) apple or wine
vinegar
1 × 15ml tbsp (1tbsp) clear honey
1 lemon
½ × 5ml tsp (½tsp) dried sage
4 pears, apples or peaches

1 Beat chops well and brush lightly with oil. Brown for 2–3 min each side on strong heat. Season.
2 Blend apple juice with vinegar, honey, lemon juice, about 1 × 15ml tbsp (1tbsp) finely grated lemon rind and sage.
3 Brush chops with mixture and cook for a further 4–5 min, with the grid 12–15cm (5–6in) away from embers. Turn chops and brush them a couple of times during cooking. Wash fruit, cut into two, and remove pips or stones. Place on the grid for the last 2–3 min.

American Spare Ribs (left)
(serves 4–5)
Preparation time: 15 min
Cooking time: 1–1½ hr
Suitable for the freezer, but will lose some flavour

1½kg (3lb) spare rib without skin
1 × 5ml tsp (1tsp) barbecue seasoning
salt, black pepper
100ml (4fl oz) oil
4 × 15ml tbsp (4tbsp) clear honey
½–1 × 15ml tbsp (½–1tbsp) wine
vinegar
2 × 15ml tbsp (2tbsp) parsley
1 × 5ml tsp (1tsp) dried rosemary or
½ × 5ml tsp (½tsp) dried lovage

1 Wipe meat well with a damp cloth. It can either be grilled whole, or parted with 2–3 bones to each piece. Rub with a mixture of barbecue seasoning and coarsely ground pepper.
2 Brush meat with a little oil, place on grid and cook for about 20 min each side on fairly strong heat. Move grid further away from coals and season meat with salt.
3 Mix together 50ml (2fl oz) oil, honey, vinegar and chopped or crushed herbs. Brush meat several times with this mixture while it cooks for another 20–50 min, turning often. The meat should be tender enough to remove bones and serve hot and sliced, with one bone on each slice. Serve with baked potatoes and grilled corn-on-the-cob (see page 55).

Marinated Pork Chops
(serves 4)
Preparation time: 10–15 min
Marinating time: 3–4 hr
Cooking time: 6–8 min
Unsuitable for the freezer

8 fairly thin pork chops
salt, pepper
Marinade:
6 × 15ml tbsp (6tbsp) oil
2 lemons
2 bay leaves
3–4 sprigs of thyme
3–4 sprigs of basil
OR 1 × 5ml tsp (1tsp) of each dried

1 Mix marinade of oil, juice of 1 lemon, 1 lemon cut in thin slices and herbs. Place chops in a deep dish and pour marinade over. Leave, covered, in a cool place.
2 Wipe marinade off chops and cook for 3–4 min each side 8–10cm (3–4in) away from embers, turn-

Left : New Orleans Chops with exciting trimmings.
Below left : Marinated Pork Chops flavoured with bay leaves, thyme and basil.

ing and brushing with marinade a couple of times. Season with salt and pepper when nicely browned.

3 Place lemon slices from marinade on the barbecue for the last few minutes of cooking time. Turn and, place on chops as garnish.

Serve with baked potatoes and a mixed green salad, or with cold potato salad and peas, beans, asparagus, tomatoes etc.

New Orleans Chops

(serves 4)
Preparation time: 10–15 min
Marinating time: about 2 hr
Cooking time: 6–10 min
Unsuitable for the freezer

4 large pork chops
1 clove garlic
salt, black pepper
Marinade :
100ml (4fl oz) oil
100ml (4fl oz) dry red wine
1 onion
pinch of cayenne
1 leek top
2 sprigs of parsley
1 sprig of thyme
Trimmings :
2 courgettes
3–4 shallots
1 leek
olive oil
1 pepper
about 200g (7oz) sweetcorn
3–4 small tomatoes
200ml (7fl oz) white stock
salt, pepper
marjoram
thyme, parsley

1 Rub chops with crushed garlic and coarsely ground black pepper. Make a couple of incisions in the fatty edge and place chops in a bowl. Mix together a marinade of oil, red wine, chopped onion, cayenne pepper, finely shredded leek green, parsley and thyme. Pour marinade

over chops and leave bowl in a cool place.

2 Wash and slice courgettes. Sprinkle with salt and place in a colander with a weight on top for about $\frac{1}{2}$ hr. Dry lightly.

3 Slice peeled shallots and cleaned leeks into thin rings. Cut pepper into cubes. Sauté these and courgettes in 1–2 × 15ml tbsp (1–2tbsp) oil on even heat. Add stock, boil for 6–8 min and mix in corn. Season with salt, pepper and herbs, and keep vegetables warm.

4 Wipe marinade off chops and barbecue for 3–5 min each side, 6–8cm (2½–3in) away from embers. Brush a couple of times with strained marinade and sprinkle a little more over chops when serving. Cut tomatoes into wedges, season with a pinch of salt, and leave on barbecue grid for a few minutes. Mix with the other warm vegetables. In addition to these vegetables, serve French bread and a green salad.

Chops with Apples and Onions

(serves 4)
Preparation time: 15 min
Cooking time: 8–10 min
Unsuitable for the freezer

4 large pork chops
oil
salt, pepper
paprika
4 firm, sharp apples
8 shallots
100g (4oz) slices of bacon

1 Make a couple of incisions in the fatty edge of chops and rub with coarsely ground black pepper and paprika.

2 Peel shallots and boil for 5 min in lightly salted water. Wash apples, quarter, and remove cores. Cut bacon slices into pieces and wrap round onions and apple wedges. Fasten with toothpicks or skewers.

3 Brush chops with oil and cook for 4–5 min each side, 6–8cm (2½–3in) away from charcoal. At the same time place onions and apples on grid and turn often. If the bacon fat dripping onto the coals catches fire, smother it immediately with water from a sprinkling bottle to avoid food getting a burnt flavour.

Serve chops with bread, Parsley Butter (see page 10) and a green salad.

Kebabs

*Kebabs are a simple yet very friendly way of entertaining.
There are many different kinds of barbecue skewers available,
but the flat-sided ones are best.*

Normandy Pork Fillet
(serves 4)
Preparation time: 15 min
Marinating time: about 2 hr
Cooking time: 8–10 min
Unsuitable for the freezer

1 × 350–450g ($\frac{3}{4}$–1lb) slice of thick
    pork fillet
2 firm, sharp apples
2 onions
salt, pepper
4 firm, boiled potatoes
Marinade :
100ml (4fl oz) oil
2 × 15ml tbsp (2tbsp) brandy or
    apple spirit (Calvados)
1 × 5ml tsp (1tsp) cider vinegar or
    wine vinegar
pinch of ground cloves

1 Trim and slice fillet. Place in
a dish and pour over well-blended
marinade. Leave, covered, in a cool
place.
2 Peel onions and cut into wedges.
Peel apples, remove cores and cut
into wedges. Thread meat slices,
apple and onion onto skewers, brush
with marinade, and place on barbecue grid 8–10cm (3–4in) away
from embers. Turn skewers often
and brush a couple of times with
marinade. Season with salt and
pepper.
3 Slice potatoes lengthways, brush
with marinade and place on grid.
Turn often, and season with salt and
pepper during or after browning.

Pork with Shallots and Mushrooms
(serves 4)
Preparation time: 10–15 min
Cooking time: 8–10 min
Unsuitable for the freezer

$\frac{1}{2}$kg (1lb 2oz) lean pork or ham
200g (7oz) shallots
250g (9oz) large mushrooms
2–3 × 15ml tbsp (2–3tbsp) oil
2 × 5ml tsp (2tsp) mustard

*Normandy Pork Fillet with apples
and onion.*

Hawaiian Ham Kebabs with fresh or canned pineapple.

1–2 × 5ml tsp (1–2tsp) lemon juice
salt, pepper
paprika (optional)

1 Cut meat into cubes.
2 Scald and peel shallots. Boil for 3–4 min in lightly salted water and drain through a colander. Peel mushrooms.
3 Thread meat, onions and mushrooms onto skewers and brush with a little mixed oil, mustard and lemon juice.
4 Grill about 10cm (4in) away from embers, turning often and brushing with remaining oil. Season with salt, pepper and paprika when cooked. Serve with wholewheat bread, or a French loaf and a herb-sprinkled tomato salad.

Hawaiian Ham Kebabs
(serves 4–5)
Preparation time: 15 min
Cooking time: 6–8 min
Unsuitable for the freezer

400g (14oz) ham or pork
1 small pineapple or 1 can
   unsweetened pineapple cubes
1 × 15ml tbsp (1tbsp) wine vinegar
1–2 × 5ml tsp (1–2tsp) clear honey
2 × 15ml tbsp (2tbsp) oil
100ml (4fl oz) port wine or sherry

1 Cut off top and base of pineapple, and cut fruit in four lengthways with a stiff, sharp knife. Place pineapple wedges on a plate and cut fruit flesh away by working a knife closely along the shell. Then cut out the hard middle core and cut fruit into cubes. Drain canned pineapple, if using.
2 Cut ham or pork into cubes and thread on skewers alternately with pineapple. Brush with vinegar mixed with honey and half the oil. Cook about 10cm (4in) away from embers, turning often.
3 Mix remaining oil with port wine or sherry, and pour over the hot skewers to serve.
Accompany with toast and a mixed green salad.

Pork Schnitzels
(serves 4)
Preparation time: 15 min
Marinating time: 1–2 hr
Cooking time: 12–15 min
Unsuitable for the freezer

4 thin slices of pork
8 or 12 small onions
8 small tomatoes
8 or 10 long, thin slices of streaky
  bacon
1 green pepper
2–3 × 15ml tbsp (2–3tbsp) oil
1 × 5ml tsp (1tsp) barbecue seasoning
salt, black pepper

1 Beat pork lightly with your hand and cut each slice into 4 or 6 pieces. Peel onions, boil for 4–5 min in lightly salted water and drain well.
2 Cut bacon slices into two and wind round onions and tomatoes. Deseed pepper and cut into strips.
3 Thread meat, onions, tomatoes and pepper onto skewers and brush with oil mixed with barbecue seasoning. Grill about 10cm (4in) away from embers, turning often and brushing with oil. Season with salt and pepper.
Serve with baked potatoes, Parsley Butter (see page 10) and a salad.

Provençale Kebabs

(serves 4)
Preparation time: 15 min
Marinating time: about 1 hr
Cooking time: about 10 min
Unsuitable for the freezer

1 × 350–400g (¾–1lb) large pork
  fillet
200g (7oz) lean, rindless bacon
4 small onions
4 tomatoes
75–100ml (3–4fl oz) olive oil
1 × 15ml tbsp (1tbsp) wine vinegar
1–2 cloves garlic
salt, pepper
paprika
1 × 5ml tsp (1tsp) dried herbs

1 Trim fillet and cut into cubes.
Peel onions and cut in half. Cut
bacon into cubes. Place all these in a
dish.
2 Mix olive oil and vinegar with
crushed garlic, ¼ × 5ml tsp (¼tsp)
coarsely ground pepper, ½ × 5ml tsp
(½tsp) paprika and herbs. Pour this
marinade over meat, bacon and
onions and leave, covered, in a cool
place.
3 Cut tomatoes in half and thread
meat, bacon, onion and tomatoes
onto skewers. Grill about 10cm (4in)
away from embers, turning often
and brushing with marinade. Season
with salt when cooked.

Shish Kebabs

(serves 4)
Preparation time: 15 min
Marinating time: 1–2 hr
Cooking time: 12–15 min
Unsuitable for the freezer

½–¾kg (about 1½lb) lamb fillet, cut
  from leg
150–200g (5–7oz) rindless bacon
salt, black pepper
Marinade:
100ml (4fl oz) olive oil
1–2 garlic cloves
1 lemon
1 bay leaf
1 sprig fresh, or ½ × 5ml tsp (½tsp)
  dried, thyme
3 sprigs fresh, or 1 × 5ml tsp (1tsp)
  dried, mint

1 Cut lamb into cubes and bacon
into slices. Place both in a bowl and
pour over marinade made by blend-
ing oil, crushed garlic, lemon juice,
finely grated lemon rind, bay leaf
and finely chopped or crushed
herbs. Leave, covered, in a cool
place.
2 Thread lamb and bacon onto
skewers and grill 10–12cm (4–5in)
away from embers, turning often
and brushing with marinade.
Finally, season with salt and pepper.
Serve with Pilaff Rice (see separate
recipe) and either a tomato, or a
simple green, salad.

Pilaff Rice

(serves 4)
Preparation time: 10 min
Cooking time: about 30 min
Unsuitable for the freezer

2–3 shallots
2 × 15ml tbsp (2tbsp) oil or butter
175g (6oz) long-grain rice
1 × 5ml tsp (1tsp) salt
¼ × 5ml tsp (¼tsp) pepper
300ml (½pt) stock
1 red pepper
150–250g (5–9oz) small mushrooms
100ml (4fl oz) dry white wine

1 Sauté chopped shallots for 5 min
in a saucepan in 1 × 15ml tbsp
(1tbsp) oil or butter. Add rice, salt,
pepper and warm stock. Stir, cover
with a tight-fitting lid, and boil for
20–25 min on very low heat.
2 Deseed pepper and cut into
cubes. Clean mushrooms.
3 Sauté pepper and mushrooms for
2–3 min in remaining oil or butter
on strong heat. Add wine, boil for
1 min, then season with salt. Mix
with the cooked rice. Serve freshly
made.

*Below: Provençale Kebabs. Right:
Shish Kebabs served with freshly
made Pilaff Rice.*

Liver and Kidneys

Calf's Liver on Skewers

(serves 4)
Preparation time: 15 min
Marinating time: 1–2 hr
Cooking time: about 10 min
Unsuitable for the freezer

½kg (1lb 2oz) calf's liver
8 shallots
12 large mushrooms
juice of ½ lemon
1 red pepper
12–16 pork, or 4 barbecue, sausages
4–6 large slices of bacon
salt, pepper
paprika
Marinade:
4 × 15ml tbsp (4tbsp) oil
2 × 15ml tbsp (2tbsp) lemon juice
1 × 5ml tsp (1tsp) mustard
¼ × 5ml tsp (¼tsp) dried marjoram

1 Slice liver and place with peeled shallots in a bowl. Mix together marinade and pour over.
2 Peel mushrooms and sprinkle with lemon juice. Wash and deseed pepper and cut into pieces. Wrap bacon round sausages.
3 Thread liver, shallots, sausages, mushrooms and pepper alternately onto skewers. Grill on a good, hot grid, turning often and brushing with marinade. Season with salt, pepper and paprika.
Serve with a French loaf or baked potatoes, Paprika Butter (see page 10) and a simple green salad.

Liver in Red Wine

(serves 4)
Preparation time: 15 min
Marinating time: 1–3 hr
Cooking time: 4–6 min
Unsuitable for the freezer

Left: Liver in Red Wine served with cold boiled potatoes in a dressing made of equal quantities of sour cream and mayonnaise. Season the dressing with a little strained marinade, salt and pepper.
Right: Liver with Bacon served with pasta and tomatoes.

8 slices calf's or ox liver
salt
Marinade:
100ml (4fl oz) red wine
3 × 15ml tbsp (3tbsp) oil
½ lemon
1 shallot
4 peppercorns
2 sprigs fresh, or ½ × 5ml tsp (½tsp) dried, thyme
3–4 sprigs fresh, or ½ × 5ml tsp (½tsp) dried, basil
1 sprig fresh, or ¼ × 5ml tsp (¼tsp) dried, rosemary

1 Mix together a marinade of red wine, oil, lemon juice, finely grated lemon rind, chopped shallot, crushed peppercorns and herbs. Pour over liver slices in a bowl and leave in a cool place.
2 Wipe marinade off liver slices and cook on barbecue grid 6–8cm (2½–3in) away from embers. Season with salt after grilling. It may be necessary to brush with more marinade. For serving suggestions, see caption to illustration.

Liver with Bacon

(serves 4)
Preparation time: 10 min
Cooking time: about 10 min
Unsuitable for the freezer

8 slices of ox or calf's liver
salt, pepper
oil
8–12 slices of bacon
fresh or dried marjoram

1 Place bacon slices on a piece of double tinfoil and turn the edges up slightly.
2 Place tinfoil across barbecue grid near embers and cook bacon slices, turning a couple of times, until crisp and golden.
3 Brush liver slices with oil, place on grid, and cook for 2–4 min each side, depending on thickness. Then season with salt and pepper and about 1 × 15ml tbsp (1tbsp) finely chopped fresh, or 1 × 5ml tsp (1tsp) crushed dried, marjoram.
Serve with boiled pasta sprinkled with parsley and a tomato salad.

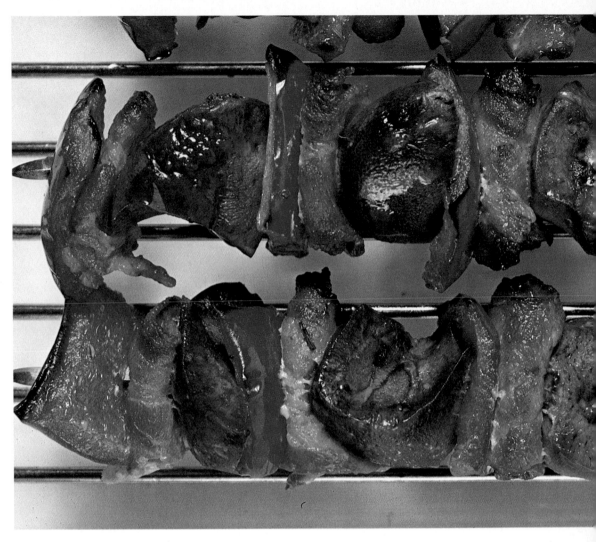

Kidneys in Garlic Bread
(serves 4)
Preparation time: 15 min
Cooking time: 8–10 min
Unsuitable for the freezer

½kg (1lb 2oz) calf's or lamb's
  kidneys
8 small onions
salt, black pepper
1 green pepper
4 bay leaves
3 × 15ml tbsp (3tbsp) oil
1 × 15ml tbsp (1tbsp) tomato purée
¼ × 5ml tsp (¼tsp) dried sage

1 Rinse and dry kidneys, remove excess fat and veins. Cut into pieces. Boil peeled onions for a few minutes in lightly salted water and drain well.
2 Wash and deseed pepper, and cut into wide strips. Thread kidney,

onions, bay leaves and pepper onto skewers.
3 Brush with oil mixed with pepper, tomato purée and sage, and cook on a hot grid, turning often and brushing with oil. Sprinkle with salt after grilling.
4 Slice open the Hot Garlic Bread (see separate recipe) and place the cooked kebabs inside. Serve with Parsley Butter (see page 10) and a green salad.

Liver Patties
(serves 4)
Preparation time: 20 min
Cooking time: 6–10 min
Unsuitable for the freezer

300g (11oz) pig's or calf's liver
250g (9oz) tender beef or minced
  beef
2 onions

1 slice of white bread
1 × 15ml tbsp (1tbsp) tomato purée
1 × 5ml tsp (1tsp) Worcestershire
  sauce
salt, pepper
paprika
oil
cress or lettuce

1 Rinse liver and remove tendons, membranes and veins. Put liver, beef in the piece, quartered onions and bread through the mincer. Mix with tomato purée, Worcestershire sauce and seasonings to taste. If you use minced beef, mix in after liver has been minced.
2 With floured hands, shape mixture into oblong rolls. Flatten a little, then brush with oil and cook on barbecue grid about 10cm (4in) away from embers. Turn patties with tongs and brush with oil to

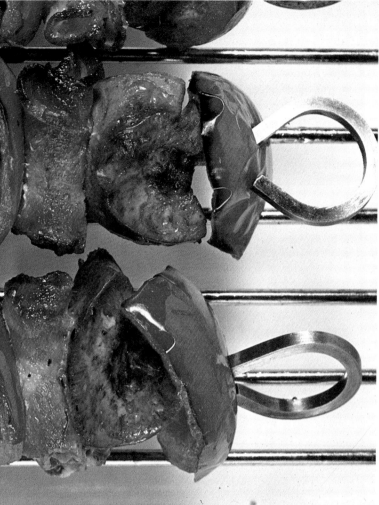

2 Cut bacon slices in half and roll up. Thread bacon rolls, slices of kidney and pieces of pepper onto skewers. Brush with oil, seasoned with black pepper and thyme.

3 Cook skewers 8–10cm (3–4in) from embers, turning often and brushing from time to time with oil. Sprinkle with salt after grilling. Serve hot with boiled rice and tomato sauce.

Hot Garlic Bread

Cut a large French loaf or 4 small French loaves nearly all the way through lengthways. Butter the cut sides with 50–75g (2–3oz) softened butter blended with 1 × 5ml tsp (1tsp) lemon juice, a pinch of white pepper and 1–2 crushed garlic cloves. Squeeze bread together and place at the edge of the barbecue grid, where the heat is not too high. Turn from time to time.

Left : Calf's Kidneys on Skewers. Below : Kidneys in Garlic Bread.

prevent them sticking to the grid. Serve on a bed of cress or lettuce leaves with white bread or Garlic Potatoes (see page 19) and Paprika Butter (see page 10).

Calf's Kidneys on Skewers

(serves 4)
Preparation time : 15 min
Cooking time : 8–10 min
Unsuitable for the freezer

½kg (1lb 2oz) calf's kidneys
2 red peppers
150g (5oz) sliced bacon
oil
salt, pepper
½ × 5ml tsp (½tsp) dried thyme

1 Rinse and dry the kidneys. Remove surplus fat and veins if any, then slice. Wash and clean peppers and cut into large pieces.

Mixed Grill

As you will see from the recipe below, a mixed grill has to be prepared carefully before you start grilling. The one who is doing the barbecuing has to be quick and alert if everything is to be ready at the same time. One or two things, however, can be grilled together.

Mixed Grill
(serves 6)
Preparation time: 25–30 min
Cooking time: see recipe
Unsuitable for the freezer

6 chicken legs
6 thin slices tender lean pork
½kg (1lb 2oz) minced beef
12 slices bacon
2–3 slices calf's liver
6 small lamb chops
6 small onions
9 small tomatoes
2 peppers (red or green)
black pepper
paprika
oil
salt, marjoram
basil, thyme

1 Dry chicken legs well, rub with pepper and paprika, and brush with oil. They are now ready for grilling.
2 Beat pork slices with your hand and rub with coarsely ground pepper and a little crushed thyme. Brush with oil.
3 Cut liver into 6–12 large cubes. Boil peeled onions for 4–5 min and cut into two or four. Cut peppers in half and slice into broad strips. Insert skewer through pieces of liver and onion, 1 rolled up slice of bacon, ½ tomato and a strip of pepper. Mix 2 × 15ml tbsp (2tbsp) oil with pepper, paprika, marjoram and basil and brush skewers.
4 Shape minced beef into 6 patties and sprinkle with pepper, paprika and a little crushed basil and thyme. Brush with oil.

5 Make a couple of incisions in the fatty edge of the chops and rub them with paprika and a little crushed thyme and marjoram. Brush with oil.
6 Halve remaining tomatoes and sprinkle with salt, pepper and basil. Brush remaining strips of pepper with oil and season with salt and pepper.
7 Grilling: First barbecue chicken legs until lightly brown on all sides and place on the outer edge of grid, where they should be ready after about 20 min. Turn often, and brush several times with oil. Season with salt when cooked. When chicken legs are nearly done, place the pork slices and the liver skewers on grid. Brown for about 2 min each side and place at the outer edge of grid. Leave for further 6–8 min, turning and brushing from time to time. Sprinkle with salt when cooked.
Last to go on the grid are the beef patties and lamb chops with the 6 remaining tomatoes, strips of pepper, and the other bacon slices. Grill everything for 2–3 min each side, perhaps a little shorter time for the bacon. Brush with oil, if necessary, and sprinkle with salt.

With mixed grill you can serve a French loaf or brown bread, a cold Green Mayonnaise Sauce (see separate recipe) and a simple green salad.

Green Mayonnaise Sauce
(serves 6)
Preparation time: 10 min
Settling time: ½–1 hr
Unsuitable for the freezer

150g (5oz) mayonnaise
200ml (7fl oz) buttermilk or skimmed milk
1 × 15ml tbsp (1tbsp) lemon juice
2 × 5ml tsp (2 tsp) light-coloured mustard
1 small onion
2 small pickled gherkins
5–6 × 15ml tbsp (5–6tbsp) finely chopped chives
chervil, tarragon, cress parsley or dill

1 Blend mayonnaise and buttermilk. Grate onion, and finely chop gherkins. Add to mayonnaise mixture with lemon juice and mustard.
2 Add finely chopped herbs as suggested above, or only one kind if you prefer. Leave sauce in a cool place before serving.

Grilled Chicken

Chicken is always tasty, either grilled whole or in pieces. If you leave the chicken in a marinade for a couple of hours before cooking, it will have an interesting and unusual flavour.

Grilled Halved Chicken

(serves 6)
Preparation time: 15 min
Cooking time: 25–35 min
Suitable for the freezer, but will lose some flavour

3 small chickens
about 100ml (4fl oz) oil
2 × 5ml tsp (2tsp) barbecue seasoning
1 × 5ml tsp (1tsp) paprika
salt
250g (9oz) shallots
about ½kg (1lb) small tomatoes

1 Cut chickens lengthways by cutting on either side of the breast bone and through it. Remove wish bone. Dry chicken well.
2 Scald and peel shallots, boil for 4–5 min in lightly salted water and drain well. Insert barbecue skewer through shallots and small tomatoes.
3 Brush chicken pieces with oil, blended with barbecue seasoning. Place on grid 12–15cm (5–6in) away from embers. Turn often and brush with oil. When the pieces have been on the grill for half the time they will take to cook, sprinkle with paprika and salt.
4 Brush tomato and onion skewers with oil and grill with chicken for the last 8–10 min of cooking time, turning and brushing often. Season with salt.
Serve with a French loaf, heated at the outer edge of grid, and Parsley or Tarragon Butter (see page 10).

Chicken Grilled Whole

(serves 4)
Preparation time: 15 min
Cooking time: 50–60 min
Suitable for the freezer, but will lose some flavour

1 large chicken
50g (2oz) cream cheese
thyme, tarragon, basil
oil
salt, pepper
1 × 5ml tsp (1tsp) barbecue seasoning
1 red pepper
1 × 397g (14oz) can peeled tomatoes
1 onion
1–2 cloves garlic

1 If frozen, place chicken loosely covered in fridge to defrost overnight. Dry well and rub inside with salt and pepper.
2 Mash cream cheese. Mix with

1×15ml tbp (1tbsp) fresh, or 1×5ml tsp (1tsp) dried, herbs and butter chicken on the inside with this mixture. Pull the loose neck skin towards the back, cross wing tips over skin and fasten with skewers. Fasten chicken to a rotating spit.

3 Brush an ovenproof, or a strong tinfoil, dish and fill with deseeded sliced pepper, coarsely chopped tomatoes, chopped onion and crushed garlic. Place dish underneath chicken and bank coals round it. Cook chicken 15–20cm (6–8in) away from embers, or in an ordinary oven with a rotating spit.

4 Mix $3-4 \times 15$ml tbsp (3–4tbsp) oil with the barbecue seasoning, brush chicken often and sprinkle with salt when nicely brown. If skin is not crisp when chicken is tender, move spit closer to the embers for the last 5 min.

5 Season vegetables just before serving. They will already have taken up flavour from the herby meat juices dripping from the chicken during grilling.

Cut chicken in four equal portions and serve with boiled rice, the barbecued vegetables and a simple green salad.

Marinated Chicken Legs

(serves 4–6)
Preparation time: 15 min
Marinating time: 2–4 hr
Cooking time: about 30 min
Suitable for the freezer, but will lose some flavour

8–12 chicken legs
salt
1 lemon
fresh mint or lemon thyme
Marinade :
1 lemon
about 100ml (4fl oz) oil
pepper
1×15ml tbsp (1tbsp) finely chopped fresh, or 1×5ml tsp (1tsp) dried, mint

1 Mix marinade of lemon juice, oil, $\frac{1}{2} \times 5$ml tsp ($\frac{1}{2}$tsp) pepper and fresh or dried mint. Pour over chicken legs, and leave in a cool place, turning from time to time.

2 If you are serving baked potatoes with the chicken, they should start cooking 20–30 min before you place the chicken on the barbecue grid. Wash and dry large potatoes and wrap in strong tinfoil. Place firmly

in the barbecue coals, until they are completely covered. Bake for about 1 hr.

3 Wipe marinade from chicken legs and put on skewers. Place on grid about 12–15 cm (5–6in) from embers, turning often and brushing with marinade. Sprinkle with salt when nearly cooked.

4 Remove potatoes with a pair of tongs (wear thick oven gloves, as the potatoes are extremely hot) and make a criss-cross cut in the top. Place chilled Parsley Butter with garlic (see page 10) in each slit.

Garnish skewers with lemon wedges and a little fresh mint or lemon thyme. Besides baked potatoes, a salad of finely shredded lettuce and slices of cucumber in an oil and vinegar dressing and sprinkled with fresh or dried mint, is a good accompaniment.

Lemon Chicken

(serves 4)
Preparation time: 15 min
Marinating time: 2–3 hr
Cooking time: about 20 min
Suitable for the freezer, but will lose some flavour

1 large chicken or 8 chicken legs
salt
lemon thyme
Marinade :
75ml (3fl oz) oil
2 lemons
$\frac{1}{2} \times 5$ml tsp ($\frac{1}{2}$tsp) pepper
1 clove garlic
$\frac{1}{2} \times 5$ml tsp ($\frac{1}{2}$tsp) ground ginger
good pinch powdered cloves

1 Divide chicken into suitable-sized pieces, or use chicken legs. Mix together a marinade of oil, juice of 1 lemon, pepper, crushed garlic, ginger and powdered cloves. Pour over chicken pieces.

2 Wipe marinade off chicken pieces and place them on the barbecue grid 10–12cm (4–5in) away from embers, turning and brushing them with marinade from time to time. Place lemon slices from remaining lemon on the grid for a moment just before chicken is ready. Place on chicken pieces, with a little fresh lemon thyme and salt, before serving. Serve with baked potatoes with Parsley Butter (see page 10), or a salad of sliced potato, peas and green beans with a lemon and oil dressing.

Fish and Shellfish Kebabs

Shrimp Kebabs (right)
(serves 4)
Preparation time: 15 min
Marinating time: 1 hr
Cooking time: 6–8 min
Unsuitable for the freezer

½–¾kg (about 1¼lb) large shrimps
    with shells or 200–300g (7–11oz)
    peeled shrimps
salt, pepper
1 lemon
100g (¼lb) bacon slices
¼ fresh, or 1 can unsweetened,
    pineapple pieces
a few fresh sage leaves or lemon
    thyme
oil
Caper Butter:
100g (¼lb) butter
2 × 5ml tsp (2tsp) lemon juice
1 × 15ml tbsp (1tbsp) capers
white pepper

1 Shell the shrimps and season with
a little salt and pepper. Squeeze
lemon juice over and leave for about
1 hr. Remove rind of fresh pine-

apple and cut into 12 small pieces, or drain canned pineapple well.

2 Cut bacon slices into smaller pieces and wrap them around all, or just some of, the shrimps.

Thread shrimps and pineapple onto skewers with a few small leaves of sage or lemon thyme. Brush pineapple pieces and shrimps without bacon with oil, and grill about 10cm (4in) away from embers, turning often.

Serve with bread, and butter or Caper Butter made by stirring the softened butter with the lemon juice, a pinch of white pepper and the small or finely chopped capers.

Cod Kebabs (below left)
(serves 4)
Preparation time: 10 min
Marinating time: 1 hr
Cooking time: 8–10 min
Unsuitable for the freezer

½kg (1lb 2oz) cod fillet
salt, pepper
1 lemon
2 × 15ml tbsp (2tbsp) finely chopped dill
4 slices smoked ham
2–3 × 15ml tbsp (2–3tbsp) oil
175g (6oz) long-grain rice
1 small can corn kernels
25g (1oz) butter
1 can mussels

1 Dry cod fillets, rub with salt and pepper and squeeze most of lemon juice over. Sprinkle with the finely chopped dill and leave in a cool place to settle for 1 hr.

2 Sprinkle rice into a saucepan containing 350ml (12fl oz) boiling water, add 15g (½oz) butter and 1 × 5ml tsp (1tsp) salt. Stir, cover with a tight-fitting lid, and simmer for 12 min on low heat. Turn off heat, but leave saucepan for at least 12 min before lifting lid.

3 Heat corn and well-drained mussels in remaining butter with salt, pepper and remaining lemon juice. Keep warm.

4 Slice cod fillet and ham into bite-sized pieces and thread on barbecue skewers. Brush with oil, grill 12–15cm (5–6in) away from embers, and turn often.

5 Mix corn and mussels with rice, and place on a hot dish with the skewers on top. Serve freshly made with Hollandaise Sauce with Chives.

Barbecued Scallops (below)
(serves 4)
Preparation time: 20 min
Marinating time: 1–2 hr
Cooking time: 4–6 min
Unsuitable for the freezer

200–300g (7–11oz) frozen scallops
250g (9oz) large mushrooms
200g (7oz) large shrimps (optional)
salt, pepper
oil
breadcrumbs
Marinade :
about 100ml (4fl oz) stock
   (water + cube)
150ml (¼pt) dry white wine
2 shallots
3 × 15ml tbsp (3tbsp) finely chopped
   parsley

1 Peel mushrooms separately, dry lightly and place in a bowl. Place defrosted, drained scallops and shrimps on top.

2 Coarsely chop peeled shallots for marinade and boil for 5 min in stock made from ¼ chicken cube to 100ml (4fl oz) water. Add white wine and parsley and bring to the boil. Cool, then pour over mushrooms and scallops and leave in a cool place.

3 Thread scallops, mushrooms and shrimps onto skewers, season with salt and pepper and brush with oil. Turn skewers in breadcrumbs and cook as directed, 12–15cm (5–6in) away from embers, turning often. Place skewers on a hot dish and pour some of the marinade over to serve.

Hollandaise Sauce with Chives
(serves 4)
Preparation time: 10 min
Unsuitable for the freezer

4 egg yolks
150g (5oz) butter
salt
juice of ½ lemon
white pepper
200ml (7fl oz) sour cream
1 sprig of chives

1 Beat egg yolks with lemon juice until light and fluffy in a thick-bottomed saucepan made of enamel, stainless steel or copper – aluminium discolours the sauce.

2 Cut butter, in thin slices, into the egg mixture. Place saucepan on low heat and stir continuously until sauce is thick and fluffy. Whisk in sour cream and flavour with salt, pepper and chives. The sauce must not be allowed to boil, or it will curdle. Pour into a heated sauce-boat and serve freshly made.

More Tempting Fish Dishes

You can barbecue fish whole or in pieces – even non-oily varieties will be juicy and tasty. These recipes have interesting ingredients and trimmings.

Barbecued Plaice

(serves 4)
Preparation time: 10 min
Cooking time: 12–18 min
Unsuitable for the freezer

4 small or medium-sized plaice
oil
lemon juice
coarse salt

1 Gut fish, but leave fins and tail. Rinse and dry, and rub well with salt.
2 Brush plaice with oil and make a few incisions in the skin to prevent them from curling during cooking. Place on barbecue grid and grill for 6–9 min each side, 10–12cm (4–5in) away from embers. Turn fish once, using an oiled palette knife or fish slice. Sprinkle fish with a little lemon juice when it is nice and brown.
Serve with a French loaf, Parsley Butter (see page 10), and a salad of tomatoes, cucumber, raw mushrooms, spinach or lettuce and finely chopped lemon thyme.

Barbecued Salmon

(serves 4)
Preparation time: 15 min
Cooking time: 8–12 min
Unsuitable for the freezer

1 small salmon, weighing about 1½kg (3lb)
oil, salt
2 lemons
200g (7oz) mayonnaise
handful of fresh spinach
50g (2oz) shelled walnuts

Small salmon or nice big trout are suitable for barbecuing. Spinach-flavoured mayonnaise with walnuts, baked potatoes and salad are tasty trimmings.

1 Gut and scrape salmon. Rub with coarse salt and dry again. A whole, frozen salmon should be defrosted slowly in the fridge or cool place overnight.
2 Cut salmon into 8 slices and dry the cut edges with kitchen paper. Brush with oil and cook on barbecue grid for 4–6 min each side, 12–15cm (5–6in) away from embers, turning once. Season with salt and sprinkle with a little lemon juice before serving.

3 Rinse spinach and run through blender with mayonnaise until spinach is finely chopped. Add 1 × 15ml tbsp (1tbsp) lemon juice and walnuts and run blender for a few seconds more. You can also chop spinach with a knife, mix with chopped walnuts and mayonnaise, and season with lemon juice and salt.
Serve salmon with baked potatoes or a French loaf, a green salad and the walnut-flavoured mayonnaise.

Trout with Herbs

(serves 4)
Preparation time: 15 min
Cooking time: about 20 min
Unsuitable for the freezer

4 trout, each weighing about 300g
  (11oz)
2 × 15ml tbsp (2tbsp) oil
juice of 1 lemon
1 clove garlic
1 × 15ml tbsp (1tbsp) tomato purée
½ × 15ml tbsp (½tbsp) fresh, or
  ¼ × 5ml tsp (¼tsp) mixed dried,
  herbs – thyme, rosemary or
  marjoram
salt, pepper
curry powder
paprika

1 Rinse, gut and dry trout, but leave head, tail and fins intact. Make small incisions at an angle in the skin on both sides and insert strong, thin sticks through the fish lengthways.
2 Mix oil, lemon juice, crushed garlic, tomato purée, salt, pepper, herbs, curry powder and paprika to taste. Brush trout with the flavoured oil and place on grid 10–12cm (4–5in) away from embers. Turn trout often and brush several times with the oil. Serve with white bread, garlic butter and a green salad.

Halibut with Aubergine

(serves 4)
Preparation time: 15 min
Cooking time: about 15 min
Unsuitable for the freezer

4 slices halibut, each weighing
  150–175g (5–6oz)
salt, pepper
juice of 1 lemon
3–4 × 15ml tbsp (3–4tbsp) oil
1 medium-sized aubergine
dill and parsley

1 Wash aubergine, cut into 2cm (¾in) thick slices and sprinkle with coarse salt.
2 Turn fish slices in lemon juice, sprinkle with a little salt and pepper and leave in a cool place for about 10 min.
Dry aubergine slices. Brush fish and aubergine with oil and cook on barbecue grid for 7–8 min each side, 12–15cm (5–6in) away from embers. Sprinkle with finely chopped dill and parsley. Serve with Parsley or Dill Butter (see page 10).

Above: Trout with Herbs. Below: Halibut with Aubergine.

Grilled Mackerel

(serves 4)
Preparation time: 15 min
Cooking time: about 20 min
Unsuitable for the freezer

2 mackerel, each weighing 500–600g
  (about 1¼lb)
salt, pepper
15g (½oz) butter
1 × 5ml tsp (1tsp) dried fennel
oil
juice of 1 lemon

1 Gut, rinse and dry mackerel, but do not remove head, tail or fins. Sprinkle insides with salt, pepper and fennel, and put a little butter in each fish. Make a few incisions in the sides.
2 Place fish in grill net or rack, and brush with oil mixed with lemon juice, salt and pepper. Cook 12–15cm (5–6in) away from embers, turning often. Sprinkle with a little lemon juice when cooked. Serve with a flavoured butter (see page 10).

Fish with Bacon

(serves 4)
Preparation time: 15 min
Cooking time: 15–20 min
Unsuitable for the freezer

allow 1 fish per person (herring,
  mackerel, etc)
juice of 1–2 lemons
salt, pepper
fresh parsley, dill and tarragon
4 slices bacon
oil

1 Gut, rinse and dry fish. Sprinkle inside and outside with some of the lemon juice and season with salt and pepper. Place a few fresh green herbs in the belly of each fish and wrap bacon slices around. Fasten with skewers or toothpicks.
2 Brush fish lightly with oil and cook on grid 10–15cm (4–6in) away from embers, turning often. Sprinkle with lemon juice when brown and cooked all the way through. Cooking time depends on the kind of fish you are using. When the flesh comes away from the backbone, is firm and not transparent, the fish is ready.
Serve with boiled potatoes sprinkled with parsley, and butter stirred with made mustard and lemon juice.

Above: Grilled Mackerel. Below: Fish with Bacon.

Grilled Vegetables

Potatoes

Wash, rinse and dry large potatoes. Cut lengthways and brush cut edges with oil. Sprinkle with salt, pepper, caraway (optional), garlic, herbs or other flavourings. You can also brush the potatoes with flavoured oil (see Barbecue Oils, page 7). Place potatoes, cut edges up, on the barbecue grid, 12–15cm (5–6in) away from the embers. Cooking time is 30 min with cut edges facing up and 5–10 min with cut edges down. Season with a little salt after grilling.

Onions

Whole, medium-sized onions should be brushed with oil and placed on the grid about 15cm (6in) away from embers. Turn onions often and allow 20–30 min cooking time, depending on size. Remove outer skin, and squeeze onion lightly to get an opening on top. Place a dab of herb-flavoured butter in opening when serving.

Aubergines (Egg Plants)

Wash and dry aubergines. Cut small ones lengthways and slice large ones. Sprinkle with coarse salt and leave for 10–20 min. Dry cut edges with paper towels, brush with lightly flavoured oil and grill for 10–15 min, according to thickness. Turn aubergines with grill tongs.

You can also grill aubergines whole by brushing with oil, and grilling for 20–30 min on the outer edge of barbecue grid. The heat should not be too strong. When the skin goes black, and the fruit feels soft, cut aubergines open and scrape out the flesh. Purée in a blender or mash with a little oil or butter. Season with salt, pepper, lemon juice, herbs, finely chopped onion, crushed garlic etc. Serve aubergine purée hot or cold with barbecued meat.

Peppers

Wash, and cut large peppers lengthways. Deseed and brush inside and outside with oil. Cook for 10–15 min on hot grid. Turn and brush often, and season with a little salt after grilling.

Tomatoes

Brush medium-sized tomatoes with oil, and grill for 6–8 min about 15cm (6in) away from embers. Turn often with grill tongs. Cut a criss-cross pattern in the top with a sharp knife when they are ready, and sprinkle salt, pepper and/or other flavourings into this when serving. Large, firm tomatoes are cut in half, brushed with oil and seasoned with salt and pepper. Grill for 2–3 min with cut edges up, brush with oil and turn. Grill for about 2 min more, closer to embers.

Fennel

Medium-sized fennel heads are washed, and sliced once or several times. Cut off the thin parts of the stalks and the green top. Brush with oil, sprinkle with salt, and grill for 10–15 min on not too hot a grill, turning often and brushing when necessary.

Corn-on-the-Cob

Only use cobs which are crisp with light yellow corns. Dark corns are not suitable, as they go mealy. Remove green leaves, if any, and the hairs inside the covering leaves. Brush the whole cob with lightly flavoured oil and grill for about 30 min. Turn often with a pair of grill tongs and brush with barbecue oil while cooking.

Courgettes (Zucchini)

Same preparation and cooking procedure as for aubergines, but do not cook for quite as long.

Other Vegetables

All vegetables can be placed on the barbecue grid wrapped in strong tinfoil. There they will be steam-boiled in their own juices – a good method for vegetables you cannot normally place on a grid, eg cabbage, asparagus, green beans, celery and peas.

Season vegetables to taste and sprinkle with a little oil or butter before squeezing the foil together, not too tightly. Cooking time will be slightly longer than when steaming in a saucepan.

Baked Potatoes

Allow 1 large potato, mealy if possible, per person. Wash and rinse well, dry, and brush skin with a little

oil. Prick a few holes in each potato with a fork, to prevent skin bursting while cooking.

You can bake potatoes on the barbecue grid with or without tinfoil, or you can wrap them in tinfoil and place between the coals. Cooking time is about 1 hr, depending on size and type. Test with a skewer to see if they are soft.

Make an incision in the potatoes and squeeze them lightly to open up the cut. Some of the potato can be removed with a teaspoon if you want to serve them stuffed.

Suggestions for Stuffing

All types of savoury butter (see page 10) go well with baked potatoes. You can also stuff them with:

● Sour cream, stired with finely chopped dill, parsley, cress, chives, tarragon, lemon thyme or other green herbs. Choose what best suits the dish you are serving the potatoes with. Add salt and pepper to taste, to the sour cream.

● Mashed cream cheese, stirred until smooth with a little cream and lemon juice, with grated onion, crushed garlic, herbs, mashed blue cheese or finely grated tangy cheese added.

● Tuna fish in oil, mashed with softened butter, lemon juice, salt and pepper.

● Black or red caviar mixed with sour cream and seasoned with lemon juice, grated onion, dill, and salt and pepper to taste.

● Equal quantities of mayonnaise and buttermilk together with finely chopped red pepper or chives or parsley, and seasoned with salt and pepper.

● Finely chopped hardboiled egg and cress stirred with mayonnaise and seasoned with curry, salt, pepper and lemon juice.

● Mashed anchovy fillets mixed with softened butter and seasoned with lemon juice and finely chopped dill.

Top : Baked Potato with stuffing.
Left : Corn-on-the-Cob and tomatoes on the barbecue grid (see recipes on page 55).

Onion and Pepper Kebabs – an ideal trimming for any meat dish.

Mushrooms on Skewers

(serves 4)
Preparation time: 15 min
Cooking time: 4–5 min
Unsuitable for the freezer

250g (9oz) large mushrooms
2 medium-sized onions
juice of 1 lemon
salt, pepper
oil
basil

1 Peel large, firm mushrooms separately under running water. Place them one by one in a colander to drain, and then in a bowl. Squeeze lemon juice over.
Peel onions and boil for 8–10 min in lightly salted water. Drain, and cut each onion into four.
2 Thread mushrooms and onion wedges onto skewers. Brush with oil mixed with a little lemon juice, salt, pepper and 1 × 15ml tbsp (1tbsp) finely chopped fresh, or $\frac{1}{2}$ × 5ml tsp ($\frac{1}{2}$tsp) dried, crushed basil. Place skewers 6–8cm ($2\frac{1}{2}$–3in) from embers, and turn often. Brush with oil to prevent skewers from sticking to the grid.
Serve with beef, veal, pork or fish.

Leeks on Skewers

(serves 4)
Preparation time: 15 min
Cooking time: 5–6 min
Unsuitable for the freezer

4 thin leeks
75–100g (3–4oz) thin bacon slices
4 medium-sized tomatoes
salt, pepper

1 Clean leeks and cut into 5cm (2in) long pieces. Boil for about 5 min in lightly salted water and drain well. Wash tomatoes, cut into four, and season with salt and pepper.
2 Cut bacon slices into pieces and wind round leek pieces and tomatoes. Thread everything onto skewers and grill about 10cm (4in) away from embers. Keep spray bottle handy in case fat from the bacon drips into embers and makes them flare up.
Serve with sausages, smoked meats, hamburgers or chicken.

Marinated Potatoes on Skewers

(serves 4)
Preparation time: 5 min
Marinating time: about 20 min
Cooking time: about 5 min
Unsuitable for the freezer

$\frac{3}{4}$kg (1lb 10oz) firm, boiled potatoes
Marinade:
3–4 × 15ml tbsp (3–4tbsp) oil
2–3 × 15ml tbsp (2–3tbsp) tomato purée
1 grated onion
salt
paprika

1 Cut cooled potatoes in two or four lengthways, depending on size, then cut into fairly thick slices.
2 Mix together marinade and pour over potatoes. Turn from time to time.
3 Insert skewers through potato slices and grill 10–12cm (4–5in) away from embers. Turn skewers often and brush from time to time to prevent them sticking to grid.
Serve with grilled meat and fish.

Onion and Pepper Kebabs

(serves 4)
Preparation time: 20 min
Cooking time: 10–12 min
Unsuitable for the freezer

200–300g (7–11oz) small red-skinned onions or shallots
1 red pepper
1 green pepper
salt, pepper
oil
wine vinegar

1 Peel onions and boil for 2–3 min in lightly salted water. Drain well. Wash and deseed peppers, and cut into fairly broad strips.
2 Thread onions and peppers onto skewers, and brush with about 2 × 15ml tbsp (2tbsp) oil, flavoured with 1–2 × 5ml tsp (1–2tsp) wine vinegar and salt and pepper to taste. Cook 12–15cm (5–6in) away from embers, turning often and brushing with oil a couple of times.
Serve with grilled beef, pork chops, chicken etc.

Grilling Indoors

Everything suitable for grilling on the outdoor barbecue can just as well be grilled in a special grill pan on the indoor cooker. You will not get the unique flavour imparted by charcoal, but the pattern from the ridges in the iron pan gives the illusion that the food has been grilled out of doors – the flavour of the raw materials and herbs will do the rest. Failing a special grill pan, an ordinary frying pan can be used.

Balkan Rolls (right)
(serves 4–5)
Preparation time: 15 min
Cooking time: about 10 min
Suitable for the freezer

½kg (1lb 2oz) minced beef
2 large onions
1–2 cloves garlic
1 × 15ml tbsp (1tbsp) flour
oil
salt, black pepper
4 × 15ml tbsp (4tbsp) finely chopped
    parsley
200g (7oz) pearl onions or shallots

1 Mix minced beef with coarsely chopped large onions, crushed garlic, flour, 1 × 15ml tbsp (1tbsp) oil, 1–2 × 5ml tsp (1–2tsp) coarsely ground pepper and parsley. Leave to settle in a cool place for about 10 min.
2 Scald and peel small onions. Boil for 3–4 min in lightly salted water and drain well. Shape mince into rolls or croquettes, and brush with oil.
3 Brush grill pans with oil and place in rolls when pan is nice and warm. Turn them carefully until they are brown all over. Place small onions in pan for the last 5 min of cooking time.
Serve with white bread or macaroni, green salad and halved tomatoes seasoned with salt and pepper.

Above left: Double Lamb Chops (see recipes on pages 28–9).

Left: Mixed Grill (see page 45).

Fireside Cookery

As described here, this is the ultimate in cosy cooking for the real barbecue enthusiast who has the right sort of fireplace well away from any carpets or furniture. If you have a burner for flambé or fondue cookery, adaptation is possible, provided you take great care or use an old-fashioned toasting fork. These recipes also provide unusual ideas for fine-weather barbecues outside.

In the Fireplace

If you are lucky enough to have a large open fireplace you can place the grid from a garden barbecue on a couple of fireproof stones, or use a grid with legs which can be placed directly above the embers.

Just as outdoors, the fire must be made ready well in advance, so that the charcoal is at the right heat and the flames have died down. You can then grill steaks, chops, sausages, chicken, vegetables and whatever else you normally grill outside. You will not get the smell of cooking in the room; that escapes up the chimney. To avoid greasy splashes, you can grill in an iron pan on the grid. It is then not important whether or not the flames have died down.

On Skewers or Forks

This type of grilling is simple to do in front of even modern types of fire, though a drip tray may be needed. Grill sausages on long skewers or toasting forks and serve with:

Sandwiches

Butter 2 slices of bread for each person and use one of the following fillings: cooked ham with mustard, thin slices of cooked liver or grilled sausages with raw onion rings, chopped hardboiled eggs mixed with a little curry-flavoured mayonnaise and finely chopped cress, cooked minced meat with tomatoes and/or onion rings, or cheese.

Place in a grill rack and cook over a fire or hot embers, turning once, until sandwiches are lightly browned and crisp.

Stick Breads

Dissolve 25g (1oz) yeast in 250ml (9fl oz) tepid water. Add 1 × 5ml tsp (1tsp) salt, $\frac{1}{2}$ × 5ml tsp ($\frac{1}{2}$tsp) oil and about $\frac{1}{2}$kg (1lb 2oz) plain flour, a little at a time, until you have a smooth dough. Allow this to rise, covered, in a warm place for 30–40 min. Knock it down, cut into 14–16 pieces, and roll these out to resemble long, thin sticks. Brush with beaten egg and bake for 15 min in an oven preheated to 200°C, 400°F, Gas 6. To barbecue, twist the long thin pieces of dough round actual sticks and cook above hot embers for 20–30 min, or until breads are done all the way through and can be loosened from the sticks.

Flambéed Chicken (above)

(serves 4)
Preparation time: 20 min
Cooking time: 40–60 min
Suitable for the freezer, but will lose some flavour

2 baby chickens
salt, pepper
butter
2 × 15ml tbsp (2tbsp) brandy
100–200ml (4–7fl oz) stock

1 Dry chickens well and rub with salt and pepper. Brown in 15–25g (1–2oz) butter in a warm pan. Sprinkle brandy over and tilt pan carefully so that the flames from the fire or burner set the brandy alight, or use a match. Shake pan until flames die out.

2 Pour a little stock into the pan and fry chickens until tender. On a barbecue, move pan and grid a notch away from the strongest heat, or cover embers with ash. Time of cooking depends on the size of the chickens. To test, insert a thin needle into thigh or breast – the juices escaping should be clear.

Serve with baked potatoes, a savoury butter (see page 10) and a green salad.

Delicious Desserts

*The barbecue usually stays
warm long after the main
course is ready and, on the
heat that remains, we can
make delicious fruit desserts.*

Vanilla Cream
(serves 4–6)

*2 eggs
2 × 15ml tbsp (2tbsp) granulated
   sugar
½ vanilla pod or 1 × 5ml tsp (1tsp)
   vanilla sugar
1 × 15ml tbsp (1tbsp) cornflour
250ml (9fl oz) milk
100–200ml (4–7fl oz) double cream*

1 Beat eggs well with sugar, crushed
vanilla pod or vanilla sugar, cornflour and milk in a thick-bottomed
saucepan.
2 Heat slowly, stirring continu-
ously, until mixture is barely boiling. Remove saucepan from heat
and stir from time to time while
mixture cools.
3 Whip cream and fold in.

VARIATION
Flavour with rum, brandy, liqueur
or chocolate instead of vanilla.

Apple
Wash whole apples, brush with oil
and place on grid over low to
medium heat. Grill for 12–15 min,
turning often. Remove core and fill
hole with butter mixed with cin-
namon, sugar and raisins soaked in
rum. Or stuff them with vanilla ice
cream.
Sliced apples with skins, but without cores, can be sprinkled with
lemon juice, brushed with oil and
grilled for a couple of minutes each
side on a warm grill. Sprinkle with
sugar and serve with whipped
cream.

Oranges and Grapefruit
Choose fruit with thick skins and
grill them whole for about 15 min,
turning often. Cut in half before
serving.
Sprinkle grapefruit with brown
sugar, oranges with a dash of orange
liqueur. Accompany with soft vanilla ice cream.

Bananas
Place ripe bananas in their skin on
the grid and turn frequently until
they feel soft inside and the skins are
black. Make a lengthwise incision,
sprinkle inside with a dash of lemon
juice, rum or brandy and eat with a
spoon.

Pears

Wash and dry firm, not too ripe pears, and brush with oil. Grill for 10–15 min on barbecue grid, turning often. Peel the warm pears, remove cores with a corer, and sprinkle with clear honey flavoured lemon juice.

Pears can also be flambéed with a little pear spirit. Sprinkle it over pears and set alight. Serve with ice-cold sour cream for a luxury dessert.

Pineapple

Slice a fresh, ripe pineapple, with the rind on, across into thick slices. Sprinkle with icing sugar and grill for 1–2 min each side on the warmest part of the grid. Turn several times to prevent icing sugar from burning.

Serve sprinkled with Madeira, brandy or liqueur (optional), and with chilled sour cream, lightly whipped cream or ice cream.

Fruit on Skewers

Choose firm fruit such as apples, pears, plums, orange wedges or firm peaches. Peel the fruit, remove cores or stones, and cut into suitable-sized pieces. Thread onto skewers, and brush with oil mixed with a dash of lemon juice. Cook on grid for about 10 min. Serve with lightly whipped cream, sour cream, vanilla ice cream or Vanilla Cream (see separate recipe).

Index